D0400147

Emotionally Healthy Teenagers

Emotionally Healthy Teenagers

Jay Kesler

WORD PUBLISHING
Nashville • London • Vancouver • Melbourne

© 1998 by Jay Kesler. All rights reserved.

No part of this publication may be reproduced, stored in a retrieval system, or transmitted in any form by any means, electronic, mechanical, photocopy, recording, or otherwise, without the prior written permission of the publisher, except for brief quotations in critical reviews or articles.

Unless otherwise noted, all Scripture quotations are from the *Holy Bible: The New International Version* (North American Edition). Copyright © 1973, 1978, 1984 by the International Bible Society. Used by permission of Zondervan Bible Publishers.

Library of Congress Cataloging-in-Publication Data

Kesler, Jay.
   Emotionally healthy teenagers / Jay Kesler.
      p. cm.
   Includes index.
   ISBN 0-8499-4069-9
    1. Parent and teenager. 2. Autonomy in adolescence. 3. Parenting.
4. Parenting—Religious aspects—Christianity. I. Title.
HQ799.15.K47 1998
649'.125—dc21   98–18431
                                                        CIP

Printed in the United States of America.

98 99 00 01 02 03 04 05 06 RRD 9 8 7 6 5 4 3 2 1

This book, more than any of the others I've written, exposes the honest, day-to-day experiences of the Kesler family, especially our children. As my son, Bruce, once said to me after hearing me preach, "You might as well use my name, Dad. After all, I'm the only son you have and so there aren't many people fooled."

I want to thank Bruce, Laurie, and Terri for their patience all these years as they have been both laboratory and illustration material. The best part is, now that they are grown, married, and have families of their own, they are making me look even better because they are living out so well the ideals we sought together. Thanks also to Celeste, Tom, and Phil, who have brought the strengths of their lives and family backgrounds to the Kesler family and have adjusted so well to our biases, which are so obvious to those who know us intimately.

I know our kids would be surprised, and even justifiably irritated, if I didn't acknowledge their mother and my closest partner in all of life, Janie, who actually followed through on all the things that excessive travel and a demanding schedule made it difficult for me to carry out.

We may have pitfalls ahead; the larger experience

would say that we will. We are committed, however, to see them through together and to glorify the Lord through our family, confident that His Word is a faithful guide in times of difficulty as well as in the routine.

JAY KESLER

Contents

Lessons from Mother Wren

Every Parent's Goal

*P*erhaps the best illustration of *Emotionally Healthy Teenagers* takes place in backyards and wooded areas all across America each year when mother wrens prepare their brood for life in a hostile and difficult world.

The Kesler family has participated in this ritual with great interest for several generations. My father taught me to build a wren house as my first boyhood project. I taught my son to build one. And last Saturday my grandson and I built five wren houses for our cottage on the lake.

Again this spring we will watch little wren families build nests, lay eggs, and hatch a batch of baby wrens who will be delighting us with their songs by summer.

When the naked little wrens become little feathered

balls, mother wren begins taking them out on nearby tree limbs where they take short trips of a foot or two. Each day their trips lengthen. After several days they not only jump from limb to limb but take some fluttering half-flights, half-jumps, and eventually short flights to nearby posts and gutters. In time they will fly greater distances, find new friends, and begin to mate. Then the cycle repeats itself. They build nests, have babies, catch insects, chirp, and sing. Before the summer is finished they will know all they need to know about being a wren and will be teaching it to their own babies.

In this simple act of nature there is a tremendous lesson for parents. Mother wren knows that her job is to teach her babies the skills they need to survive in a hostile environment. She does not hold class on mornings when the neighborhood cat is on the prowl. In fact, it is virtually impossible to get wrens to nest in an area where there is a prowling cat. If a cat lives a few houses away, mother wren watches its every move and holds class while the cat is catching up on his sleep after a night of prowling.

Mother wren is very aware of the dangers to the little birds and allows them freedom only when there is no danger. However, as they grow older, she involves them in her scolding as she hops from limb to limb, taunting the hungry cat on the ground below. Part of growing up is to learn there is such a thing as an enemy, to recognize it, and to warn others of its presence.

This instinctive behavior is a good model for parents to follow. Quite frankly, there are neighborhood cats in the world today that pose great danger to our young people. The purpose of this book is to help parents build independence and awareness into their offspring, just as mother wren does every spring.

In the very early years of parenting, our children are totally dependent on us. In this they are not like the wrens, because they remain dependent much longer. A wren has no need for its mother after a few weeks. A human baby at that age is totally incapable of surviving on its own. Because our children are dependent on us for so long, we begin to gain our own meaning in life from the relationship we enjoy with them. This, of course, is one of the great rewards of parenting. The sense of warmth you feel when a small child crawls onto your lap and falls asleep in your arms. The softness of the baby's head against your cheek. The pleasure of quietly reading a story to a child and explaining the very basic wonders of his or her newly discovered world.

"The goal of parenthood is not to maintain dependence, but to take on the difficult and demanding task of nurturing independence."

These experiences are good for the parent as well as for the child, but they are seductive. We can become dependent on them. I am not saying this dependence is always a neurosis, but it can become one if a second stage of growth doesn't take place within the mind of the parent.

The second stage is a transitional period when parents intentionally move away from this rewarding, satisfying, even dependent relationship with a child in which personal meaning is enhanced by the child's need.

Let's face it, the need to be needed is a very strong, very basic human desire. Many a father and mother get up and go to work day after day not because of the sheer excitement of the workplace but because their son needs shoes or their daughter needs school clothes. Most parents do this willingly and without resentment, and they feel a certain sense of pride and accomplishment when they do it well.

There is a time, however, when parents need to back off and realize that the goal of parenthood is not to maintain this dependence, but to take on the difficult and demanding task of nurturing independence.

This book is not about a moment in time; it is about the processes that must take place to prepare young people to cope in the world apart from their parents. In the natural world, we call this the weaning process.

I suppose everyone who has observed it in nature has thought of it as a cruel process. It is a sad sight to watch a mother lion at the zoo slap a lion cub and knock him end over end for trying to nurse when nursing is no longer appropriate. There will be a bit of crying and pain as she teaches him to act like a mature lion instead of a dependent cub.

This weaning process in the animal world is quicker and less complicated than in human beings, but it is the same concept. A child weaned from his mother's breast or a bottle is not truly weaned. That is just the first of many stages. The weaning process continues throughout the teen years, until the child is completely independent of both parents.

I don't know whether wrens return to the wren house to find out how their mom put the nest together. I suspect they don't. Nor do I think they bring their little brood back to the original house so mother wren can see her grandbabies.

In the human world, however, one of the last stages of the nurturing process is the reward stage. When children develop independence, they willingly come back to the nest. They seek continued nurturing and advice to understand how to live in the adult world.

With all of our children grown now, and with nine grandchildren, Janie and I are rewarded by the fact that all of our children are coping very well. They are working through the difficulties and struggles of parenting successfully, yet they do come back for counsel now and then.

Time marches on and sooner or later we will no longer be accessible to our children. Therefore, it is necessary for us to acknowledge this time line and plan for the future.

Last night I watched Taylor University students participate in a track meet. I particularly enjoyed watching the relays because they involve the cooperative effort of four runners. As I watched them come around the track, I realized that one of the most important parts of the race is the passing of the baton. Most of the races are won or lost in this effort. Those who pass it smoothly and without hesitation usually win the race.

––·–·–·–·–·–·–·–

"The ten principles in this book won't eliminate all the sadness of letting go, but they will help you to manage it."

––·–·–·–·–·–·–·–

The same is true of parents. Those who pass the baton smoothly and without hesitation to their children enable their kids to finish the race of life in good standing.

One of the more humorous situations played out repeatedly in my office involves the young family whose firstborn is getting ready to go to college. Dad will sit in one chair, mother and son will sit on the couch, and I will pull my chair up to form a small circle and then begin the conversation.

"Tell me a little about yourself," I say. "Where do you live? Oh, Grand Rapids. I know someone who lives there." And so on it goes.

After completing the small talk, I turn my attention to the prospective student and try to get him to respond to me. After all, he is the one I will be dealing with for the next four years. He'll be living in our dorms, interacting with our students, and taking up a place in our classrooms. I have to find out if he's going to use our resources wisely.

If the son does not answer my questions to the parents' satisfaction, his mother and father will start finishing his sentences for him. "Remember, you also did quite well in English," or "Tell Dr. Kesler about winning the speech contest."

The boy will be hesitant. He's not sure he wants to tell me as much as I want to know, and he's not completely comfortable talking to adults. So the parents take over the conversation as if he is a lump of clay sitting there with no voice or opinion.

To get the young man back in the conversation, I move my chair directly in front of the son. Then I look him directly in the eye and continue to talk to him. Sometimes I find myself with my back almost totally to the mother and dad and with my body squared off toward the son to block the parents out of the conversation. This gets a bit comical, of course, and I wonder why it takes them so long to figure out that I'm trying to get their son to take responsibility for his own answers. I want him to have the privilege of building his history with me on his own terms.

Sending kids off to college is one of the major transitions in the life of a family. To give it proper recognition, our school has a commissioning service where the faculty accepts from the parents the responsibility of taking over the lives of their children.

The liturgy includes prayers and Bible readings. The faculty and administrators officially accept the responsibility given to them by parents. Parents vow to maintain contact with us and with their kids. And the young people commit themselves to their parents, to us, and to God, pledging that they are entering this process in good faith.

It is a beautiful service. There are many tears, but they are tears of goodness and love, not tears of disappointment, sadness, rejection, or sorrow.

I am not sure how deeply mother wrens feel when their babies leave the nest, but I know that human moms and dads feel it very deeply.

The ten principles in this book won't eliminate all the sadness of letting go, but they will help you to manage it. When teenagers are properly prepared for adulthood, parents can let them grow into it with a lot less fear and reluctance. This book will help you to teach your offspring the lessons mother wren teaches hers: to recognize danger, avoid it, and show others how to do it as well. And beyond that, this book will help you to teach your children to distinguish right from wrong and to develop the strength of character to choose what is right.

Through this process remember that the goal—an emotionally healthy teenager—is reached over time. It requires effort and faith on the parts of the parents and the teens, and most important, God's help. Ask for it often.

1

The Look of
Love

PRINCIPLE 1

Love your spouse more than your kids.

*A*fter Janie and I had one of our first meals together as husband and wife, I got up from the table, walked around to where she was sitting, thanked her for the meal, and told her I loved her. At that moment it dawned on me that my father had finished every meal exactly that way. Without saying a word to me, my father had taught me that husbands were supposed to behave that way with their wives.

As a small boy, I often saw my own parents show affection for each other and I always felt very secure about it. Only after I was married, however, did I realize how deeply this had been ingrained in me. To have this tradition in one's family is a marvelous thing.

The primary relationship between a husband and

wife is the foundation on which kids build their sense of security, their identity, and learn to relate to others. This prepares them to eventually relate to their own spouse. Couples are virtually helpless in relating to one another in later life if they have not observed a healthy relationship between their own parents. In fact, it is only through a great deal of effort and relearning that people are able to overcome a dysfunctional family life. Therefore I repeat: The relationship between husband and wife is primary. When a couple become estranged but stay together because "the kids need us," the family is in real trouble.

There is a good deal of evidence to indicate that most couples make the right choice when they choose a marriage partner. Compatibility and temperament tests done on troubled couples usually verify that they are well suited for one another. But something went awry. Therefore, from the very beginning of marriage, couples need to tenaciously protect the urges and attractions that brought them together in the first place.

Think back to the earliest stages of courtship when you fell in love and couldn't stand being apart. You spent hours talking or just being together enjoying one another's presence. You would say good-bye on the front porch, go to the car, return to the porch, and go to the car again—back and forth, until your parents thought you had lost your senses.

After marriage, however, distractions crept in.

Although they were mundane and ordinary things, they robbed you of the ecstasy of new love. You faced the challenges of a career, sometimes two careers. You had problems adapting to employers and their demands. You got caught up in your own appetites, desires, and the lure of success and all its trappings: cars, houses, furniture, and clothing. If you weren't careful, these things began to consume your energies. Very few couples analyze what's happening. They just let it happen.

In homes like this teenagers feel as if they are living in an earthquake zone. As Mom and Dad grow farther and farther apart, they fear that the plates of the earth are going to separate and they will drop through one of the crevices. This adds pressure to the already turbulent world of adolescence that they face.

———————————

"The relationship between a husband and wife is the foundation on which kids build their sense of security, their identity, and learn to relate to others."

———————————

So it is my counsel that you first of all protect and nurture your relationship with one another, loving one another supremely, not allowing house, furniture, kids, career, or anything to separate you. This seemingly selfish act provides the climate that can best assure the happiness and welfare of your children.

Some of the best money you can spend is for a

weekend away with your spouse. Taking uninterrupted time to be together and to cultivate your relationship is a powerful investment.

Teenagers need to understand that Mom and Dad have something special going. They need to see you touch each other, kiss each other, show affection for one another. They need to know that your marriage is solid and that there is nothing anybody can do to divide you from one another. They've got to know that your relationship is strong enough to last forever.

Only from a relationship this strong can you communicate to your teens that you love them. When children see that you are able to maintain this kind of relationship with each other, that you are able to love each other even through disagreements, disappointments, and failure, they will believe that you are able to love them with the same unconditional love.

A solid relationship with your spouse will say to your children, "We love you dearly, and we are going to be loyal to you. *And* we are going to be consistent in our discipline and united in our opinions. There is nothing to be gained by trying to drive a wedge between us because it cannot be done. We are united in our love for each other and our love for you."

This solid relationship between husband and wife

is a foundation stone on which teenagers build their concepts of love, fidelity, loyalty, trust, confidence, authority, assurance, and a whole range of human values that we cannot communicate with words alone. It is where a healthy emotional life begins for teens.

2

Who's the Boss?

PRINCIPLE 2

Expect obedience; don't beg for it.

*H*ardly a day goes by that I don't see a parent pleading with a child to obey. When parents allow their kids to argue about every order or assignment, there is an authority problem in the family and it doesn't necessarily belong to the children. Unfortunately, when parents negotiate with children when they are young, the kids grow up to become masters at trying to manipulate every situation. In addition to the fact that this makes the teen years exasperating for parents, it is guaranteed to make the teens' adult lives more difficult.

There are plenty of parents who either have refused to accept the authority that goes with having children or have not realized they are supposed to take it. In

the real world the law of cause and effect is opera-
tive. Employers, policemen, Internal Revenue Service
representatives, college deans, viruses, and cholesterol
have one thing in common: They follow predeter-
mined rules that, if bent or broken, have consequences.
Parents do their teens no favors by always providing
a safety net or adjusting every time line, household
chore, or request to fit the teen's convenience. Expect
to be listened to and obeyed; and if not, there must
be some commensurate penalty, inconvenience, missed
reward, or disapproval to make disobedience in some
way less pleasant than if compliance had been the
response. Knowledge that there will always be dis-
pleasure at disobedience or what kids call "attitude"
will cause forethought. *Consistency* is the watchword.
As you think back to your own teen years, what teacher
did you appreciate and respect? It was always the one
who had high expectations and consistent demands,
not the one students manipulated and conned to give
in to their demands.

During the sixties all authority came under question, and today we are living with the consequences.
Although respect for authority died three decades ago,
authority itself did not. The world is still set up in such
a manner that God, as Creator, has authority over it,
and He has given parents authority over their children
so they will learn respect and obedience from a loving source.

Young children know instinctively that someone has to be in control, and they figure "Why not me?" When a parent stumbles at all in this area, questioning even for a moment his or her own authority, children jump at the chance to step in and take over. If this happens regularly, the parents may as well say, "Look, being the authority is too much trouble, so whenever it's easier for me, you can be your own authority." One of the many problems with this scenario is that the child is somehow supposed to read the parent's mind and know who's in charge of every different situation. This, of course, is impossible and leads to the kind of scene we see so often in public places: parents begging for obedience.

Your own children learned early whether or not you expected them to obey the first time you spoke or not until the second or third time or when you lost your temper and started screaming. If you expected to be obeyed the first time you spoke, discipline began immediately if obedience didn't. You knew your children were bright. Patience, repetition, and consistency were all it took for them to learn what you expected.

A teenager who never learns to accept authority without trying to negotiate will have problems later in life. When young people like this arrive at college thinking they can negotiate every single issue, they quickly become disillusioned and usually angry. If they do their first term paper "their way" for a crotchety

professor who has demanded for thirty years that every
term paper look exactly alike, they will learn that the
consequence of disobedience is a failing grade. I meet
a lot of young people these days who seem to believe
that authority has no place in the world, that every
principle is up for grabs, that every rule is negotiable.
It is unfortunate, to say the least, that their parents
didn't teach them otherwise.

The strongest tool with teenagers is an understanding of their greatest and deepest desire: being
treated like an adult. They want desperately to be independent and trusted. Though they might not enjoy a
word study, the key is in the word *trustworthy*. When
a teen says, "I feel like I am being treated like a baby,"
the parental response should be, "I can understand
that. Let's talk about how you can show us you are
ready to be trusted. In a couple of years you will want
a driver's license and be out on your own at games
and other activities. Here are the things that we notice
that will help you to show us you can handle more
independence: We expect you to keep your word.
We expect you to call us if you are going to be late.
We expect you to go where you tell us you are going
so we can find you in an emergency. We expect you
to handle your time well so that we don't have to nag
you to get your studies done. We expect you to be
considerate of the rest of the family. These are the
things adults do without thinking. You will do all of

these things and more when you are an adult—in the meantime we want to help you learn to handle freedom and as you are able, we will let loose and you will have all the freedom you will ever want."

Every once in a while during a college discipline situation a parent will stubbornly insist to me that his or her child is truthful even when others' accounts contradict him. I am always gratified when the parent says, "I know my son or daughter and because we've been through many experiences during the teen years, I'm confident of him now." This is the acid test. It doesn't just happen. This kind of parent-teen trust is established in early adolescence. We start when they are younger and expectations are modest so that in college they have established their integrity.

It is important for teens to know that we have certain expectations of them but that we will be reasonable when they fail and help them do better next time.

Parents are the ones who decide what the expectations of the household will be. They decide whether the kids or the adults will clean their bedrooms, whether the kids or the adults will put the dirty clothes in the hamper, whether people are allowed to leave wet towels on the bathroom floor or expected to hang them on the rack.

Expectations aren't reached just because we set them, of course. They're reached because we know that enforcing them is part of the long and important task of parenting, and we do so with consistency. If we help teenagers reach relatively inconsequential expectations, the larger ones will be much easier for them to reach as they become adults.

Much of the battle is won at an early age, yet there is more training to do when your children reach their teens. For example, teens should learn to handle money by budgeting their allowance or earnings. They should be encouraged to save for larger items and understand the trade-offs that determine the family's life style. Writing the family checks and balancing the checkbook for a couple of months teach young people why Mom and Dad sometimes must say no to certain demands. Helping to care for the home and carrying a fair share of household duties—including lawn work, window washing, dishes, laundry, ironing, and vacuuming—build a sense of appreciation for parents and keep teens from taking these things for granted. Learning skills so basic as ironing a shirt or blouse, loading a washer, and checking the oil in the car will save a lot of strain when they go to college or move out on their own.

It is amazing to me that, for whatever reason, many kids arrive at college unable to perform these basic tasks and oblivious to the fact that someone has been taking care of these details for them. I suspect that somehow their parents just found it easier to do these things than to put up with the hassle of teaching them.

Granted, these are not issues on which the fate of the world hangs. But we are not talking about the fate of the world; we're talking about raising emotionally healthy teenagers, whose fates are very important indeed.

— 3 —

Whose Side
Are You On?

PRINCIPLE 3

Work with your kids, not against them.

We have reached a new stage in the life of our family. Our kids no longer make fun of Janie and me when we get out the old family photo albums. In fact, they're usually the ones to get them out when they are home together.

After their own kids are in bed, they will sit for hours and look at the albums. Every once in a while one will giggle and laugh and point at a picture, recalling some special memory the photo evokes. Frequently, this leads them to tell us things we didn't know were going on behind the scenes (and frankly, we're glad we didn't know).

These old photos do more than take me on a quiet stroll down memory lane. They help me see parenting from a different perspective. They show me how important it is for parents to be aware of the physical and emotional changes and challenges that are shaping a child's self-image and to respond appropriately.

For instance, I noticed in some of the pictures how pudgy our oldest daughter was as a baby. She reminded us of the child in the Campbell's Soup ads. We laughed about how fat she was and people commented on how healthy she looked with her chubby, rosy cheeks. However, when I look at that photo along with one of her as a sixth grader, I remember a very meaningful conversation the two of us had. We had built a new house in another neighborhood, so the children would be changing schools. Laurie and I were driving over to the new house before we moved and she said, "You know what, Dad? I have decided to be a whole new person when I get to our new school."

"What do you mean by that?" I asked.

"Well, people just think about you in a certain way when you have been with them a long time, and all the kids think of me as a certain kind of person, but I am going to be different when I get to the new school."

"What do you mean?" I asked again, starting to get a little concerned.

"Well, I am going to do some things I never did before. I am going to get involved in things I wasn't involved in, and I am going to be a lot more fun at the new school."

Then I recalled how she had struggled with her self-image. She carried her pudginess into first and second grade, and I am sure her friends said cruel things to her about her weight, making her feel rejected.

I credit Janie for providing the example and encouragement to help her lose weight with proper diet and nutrition. A mother whose precious baby girl is of the Campbell's-Soup-kid variety knows that chubbiness will not be considered cute as she approaches her teen years. So Janie began to help Laurie with her diet. It was not a matter of talking about it or expecting her to do it alone. It was something we all worked on together. We learned a different way of cooking, a different way of eating, and a different way of thinking about food and exercise.

"It is for parents to be aware of the physical and emotional changes and challenges that are shaping a child's self-image and to respond appropriately."

As a result, Laurie did not feel picked on or separated from the family. She simply followed her mother's example and became a young woman very different from what she would have been if her mother had been careless.

By the sixth grade, she had lost her baby fat but

she had not lost the emotional scars left by the rejection. She determined to change all that—to leave behind those old harmful feelings and indeed she did. She became a much happier person, made more friends, and in general was much better adjusted socially at the new school.

Something similar happened with our son. When I look at his pictures I remember something of the struggle he had. He looked like the little boy called Froggie in the *Our Gang* movies. Froggie wore glasses much too big for his face, and that is the way Bruce looked when he was little. He had one eye that wandered so he had to wear very strong, and bulky, corrective glasses.

Not only were the glasses too big in size, they were too big in the proportion of time and responsibility they required. Those glasses became one of the main topics of conversation in our family. "Don't break your glasses, Bruce." "Have you forgotten your glasses, Bruce?" "Where are your glasses, Bruce?" "Push your glasses up, Bruce." "When are you going to clean your glasses, Bruce? I can't even see your eyes through the dirt." "Son, can't you learn to put your glasses where they belong so you can find them?"

As a result of kids who teased him and parents who nagged him, Bruce developed a temperament that wasn't healthy for a young boy. He became hesitant to get involved with other boys, and he particularly avoided any activity that required physical contact because he was afraid he'd get into trouble for breaking his glasses.

Finally Janie and I had a long conversation about the personality traits he was developing. "Let's stop worrying about whether he breaks his glasses or loses them," I suggested. "Let's let him spend more time with his friends. I'm sure they're getting into mischief. But let's put up with a little bit to see if Bruce will come out of his shell."

And he did. His eyesight eventually was corrected with surgery, but he grew out of his unhealthy self-consciousness even before discarding his glasses because he became less conscious of his limitations.

Our youngest daughter's pictures confirm how important it is for parents and children to work together in the growing-up process. Terri had extremely crooked teeth. Though she had a wonderful personality and everyone considered her cute, her teeth obviously needed straightening.

I remember going to the orthodontist's office and talking to him about her problem. He had her bite on a piece of clay so he could make a mold of her teeth. He would make another one after he finished his very expensive task to show us the improvement. Although I never questioned the validity of the procedure, I was extremely alarmed at the cost. Other than buying our house, it was the largest financial commitment we had

ever made. Yet we wanted to do it for Terri, and she
wanted it done too.

> **"Whether it's a weight problem, a bad
> habit, or a learning disability, teenagers
> need their parents working with them to
> help them change it or overcome it. It
> takes effort and commitment from both
> parties to end up with a beautiful result."**

The commitment involved more than just our money.
It involved pain, patience, and perseverance on Terri's
part as well. The orthodontist had to remove several
of her teeth before he could begin to line up the others. As she endured the pain and carefully followed
all the doctor's directions, we paid the bills. Our com-
bined commitment eventually paid off. After looking
at years of school pictures showing wires wrapped
around her teeth, finally there is one showing a beau-
tifully transformed smile.

For me, this experience symbolizes the process kids
and parents go through. Whether it's a weight problem,
a bad habit, or a learning disability, teenagers need their
parents working with them to help them change it or
overcome it. It takes effort and commitment from both
parties to end up with a beautiful result.

There are a thousand stories, a thousand lessons, in every family album. The point of this exercise is to get you thinking about your family in a different way, looking at it from a different angle. Look at the kids when they were small and see what their activities, dress, facial expressions, and position in the photo tell you about them and especially about their self-esteem. Ask yourself what you could be doing to help them improve their self-image. This is crucial in these years when hormones rage and sensitivity reaches an all-time high.

For instance, is there one child who never wants his picture taken, who always avoids the camera? Is he completely absent from the photos or does he only show up with his back turned or his hand over his face? Can you think of a reason your son doesn't want his picture taken? Does he have problems with his weight or complexion?

A boy with acne doesn't develop it overnight. It comes on gradually, and family members can get so used to it that they no longer even see it. Although it is good that the family accepts him, you need to realize that this may be the greatest single personal problem your son is struggling with. When you think he is moody, irritable, uncooperative, and hates the family, he may instead be embarrassed by his appearance. Does he seem withdrawn, spending all of his time in his room listening to music with the volume turned up to a deafening decibel? Perhaps this is a signal that he does not want to face the world because he doesn't feel accepted. A teenager like this needs help, not condemnation, from his parents. He needs someone to assure him that he will overcome this problem. And he needs parents who will do everything they can to help him overcome it.

Among the unending list of popular psychology books was one written several years ago titled *Psycho-Sybernetics* by Maxwell Multz. In it he talked about his discoveries as a plastic surgeon. People often came to him convinced there was something wrong with the look of their face. Their noses were too large, their eyes were shaped wrong, their chins receded too much, or some other feature made them dissatisfied with their appearance.

Although Dr. Multz found their looks fit well within the range of normal and acceptable, they couldn't be convinced. So he would do minor surgery on whatever feature they disliked, and the patient would have an entire personality change based on his or her new sense of acceptability. Dr. Multz concluded that we are the kind of people we perceive ourselves to be.

I am not advocating cosmetic surgery for every minor defect; I am just illustrating how important perceptions are and stressing the importance of the parents' role in shaping these perceptions.

"Teens taught to focus on failure rather than success will spend their lives looking at the hole without ever seeing the doughnut."

The view teenagers have of themselves—smart or stupid, trustworthy or unreliable, good-looking or ugly, gifted or hopeless, ornery or charming—is largely transferred to them by parents.

Teens need parents who have confidence in them, parents who say, "You can make it. We believe in you." People learn to overcome failure when it is looked on not as a disqualifying mark that is carried throughout life but as an experience to build on. Thomas Edison failed a thousand times to find the right element for the incandescent light bulb. But finally he tried tungsten. In reality, each failure is a kind of success because it teaches us one of a thousand ways that don't work.

Young people need to be nurtured in an environment that allows them to try new things and see how well they can do, to laugh at their mistakes and try again, to look at imperfect performances of the past and see improvement. Teenagers raised in an atmosphere of affirmation are likely to be healthier, have better self-esteem, and achieve more in life than those raised in an atmosphere that continually says, "You screwed up again; you will never amount to anything." Teens taught to focus on failure rather than success will spend their lives looking at the hole without ever seeing the doughnut.

To a great degree, the parental task is to observe each child and come up with an individualized approach to help each one. This applies to discipline and guidance as well as to developing a self-image.

There are those who argue for evenhandedness and fairness in a way that seems to indicate parents should treat each of their offspring exactly the same way. Every parent should, of course, strive for justice and never play favorites. However, there is no way that each child can be treated exactly the same because no two children are alike.

Kids and teenagers do not need equal amounts and types of discipline any more than both need a shot of penicillin if only one has a sore throat. Discipline and correction must be meted out in an overall climate of fair play, affirmation, and love. However, there is no Bill of Rights for families and no library of legal documents to refer to. Effective discipline requires wisdom and creativity.

One of the most inspiring teens I have ever known shared his story with me. He began his life as an abandoned child with a muscular disorder that necessitated his using crutches so he could half walk, half drag himself along. He told me of how he arrived at the house of his adoptive parents loaded in the car with four or five other adopted kids who were to be his family. All had some kind of physical handicap, some more severe than his own. When they stopped at the curb, everyone jumped out of the car and climbed the several steps onto the porch, leaving him standing there alone, wondering how he would ever get into the house. His new parents and all of his new siblings were waiting, though. They stood on the porch yelling encouragement to him, clapping their hands, whistling, and singing, "Come on, you can do it!" He recalls that he walked, stumbled, crawled, crept, walked again, climbed, struggled, and finally made the last step. His new family jumped all over him like a hockey goalie who'd just won the game and kissed and hugged him as he had never experienced before. Then his new parents said, "Welcome to your new family. As you can see, we all have our problems but we love each other and we help by doing what we can do ourselves before we ask others to do it for us."

This teenager is now a young man working with troubled youth in a Christian ministry. He is profoundly grateful that wise parents taught him self-reliance, even though there was considerable discomfort and pain, so that he can be a useful, fulfilled adult. He is, in my opinion, sometimes a little harsh with his young clients but they know by watching him that he knows what he is talking about. His parents are still taking on other challenged children like him and prayerfully adapting love to fit each individual need.

"If parents ridicule or criticize people with faults or disabilities, children will learn that every imperfection makes people, themselves included, undesirable."

Though few of us must deal with these extreme challenges, many do, and in my experience they do it better than the rest of us because there is no way to cop out or to pretend that the reality is not there.

This young man's parents, like experienced teachers, know that the tone of voice, the lift of the eyebrow, the sense of trust and expectation can be the determining factor in their children's lives. My experience would say that most young people will break their backs not to disappoint us in our high opinion of them. It is my view that we should tell them of our dreams for them and put stars in their eyes rather than throwing cold water on their aspirations, even if they seem rather lofty by our adult and often jaded estimation.

"Wise parents acknowledge imperfections, improve the ones that are correctable, and find ways to overcome or compensate for those that are not."

Likewise, what the parent conveys through verbal and nonverbal communication will determine a teen's self-image. If parents ridicule or criticize people with faults or disabilities, their teenagers will learn that every imperfection makes people, themselves included, undesirable. On the other hand, parents who accept and love others despite their imperfections will help their kids grow up accepting their own.

Wise parents acknowledge imperfections, improve the ones that are correctable, and find ways to overcome or compensate for those that are not. And by doing so, they help their children do likewise and become emotionally healthy teens.

— 4 —

Youth and Consequences

PRINCIPLE 4

Teach your teen the concept of cause and effect.

*F*or teens nurtured on TV and movies, reality and fantasy are all mixed up. In a one-hour television program, the hero may be shot with an assault rifle, have several bones broken in the fight, and be out of the hospital and back in action by the end of the hour.

Parents can do little to change modern culture, so what can they do to instill in teenagers a healthy sense of reality? The only way I know to do this is to make sure our teens understand the consequences of their own actions, and this requires a response from parents that is swift, sure, and appropriate. By *appropriate* I mean that the reaction fits the teenager's misbehavior, or, in other words, that it teaches true consequences.

If in a moment of exasperation a parent says, "Okay, you are grounded for a month," it will be hard to enforce the threat. It would be better to say, "I've decided that you cannot go to the game and fifth-quarter party Friday night to help you understand that this is serious and cannot become a pattern of behavior."

In such a case it is not wise to let other friends come to your house and turn the discipline into a party. Sometimes I wish people still read Brer Rabbit stories in order to understand the principle. Brer Fox always lost when Brer Rabbit said, "Oh please, Mr. Fox, don't throw me into the brier patch," which, of course, was his natural habitat. A teenager in his or her room with a computer, CD player, and television probably won't learn too much from being grounded. Cleaning the garage or basement may be remembered a little longer.

Sometimes the only way to make teenagers understand is to expose them to the disappointment and pain associated with a certain behavior.

Few activities associated with the teen years are more fraught with frustration and anger than driving. Reminders to get the oil changed, to replace a burned-out taillight, or to fix a noisy muffler are often ignored or put off because they take time, cost money earmarked for concert tickets, or are just plain troublesome. At some point the lesson is better learned if a traffic citation is issued or a costly engine repair is required. A disabled car sitting in the driveway may teach more than a nagging dad can accomplish by becoming hoarse or raising his blood pressure. Of course, if the father relents and pays the ticket or repair, he gets both, as well as losing the chance to teach responsible behavior.

Sometimes, to teach a particular lesson, we even have to allow kids to do things that seem foolish. Clothing is a good example.

"Teens whose parents bail them out every time they make bad judgments learn that bad decisions are really good ones because someone is always there to undo the consequences."

When a kid wants to buy a pair of shoes that costs four times the amount of a pair without the brand-name label, it may be good to give him a clothing budget and let him buy what he wants. No matter how much it grates against your sense of good judgment, let him spend it all on one pair of shoes if that's what he decides to do. After he's made the choice, however, don't give in and buy him jeans to go with the shoes, no matter how pathetic he looks when he has to wear last year's clothes. If you give in, you haven't just lost an opportunity to teach a good lesson, you've taught a bad one.

Teens whose parents bail them out every time they make bad judgments learn that bad decisions are really good ones because someone is always there to undo the consequences.

Refusing to let kids make decisions is just as bad, perhaps worse, than not allowing them to suffer the consequences of bad decisions. Young people who are unable to make their own choices or form their own opinions on issues and matters of life style usually have been overprotected, in some ways debilitated, by well-meaning but unwise parents who were afraid or unwilling to let their kids suffer the consequences of bad decisions. So afraid, in fact, that they didn't allow them to make any decisions at all.

Apparently that was the route chosen by the mother in Alfred Hitchcock's movie *Psycho*. Hitchcock scared viewers silly with his story about a woman who made her son so dependent on her that when she died he kept her body, dressed it, and propped it in a chair so he could consult her about every decision. Although the movie portrayed an extreme case, many people, after watching the film, thought of someone who reminded them of Norman—someone so dependent on a parent, so afraid of the consequences of making a mistake, that he or she became dysfunctional when the parent was no longer available to make decisions.

To keep teenagers emotionally dependent by refusing to let them make decisions or by protecting them from bad ones is to fly in the face of the entire created order. In all areas of God's creation He allows His creatures to mature and function on their own. To participate with God in His creation we must, therefore, prepare our children for independence, for that is consistent with His plan. In a sense, we are carrying out His will and His intentions when we do so.

Reasons for not doing this vary. Some parents fear that their teens are inadequately prepared and will fail and be hurt. Others simply lack faith. They are unable to trust their young people to God's protection and feel they must provide it themselves. In essence, this is a refutation of God's promise that our times are in His hands.

Some parents have inadvertently developed a codependent relationship with their children. They need to have their kids depend on them. They get their meaning for life from this dependence and therefore encourage it and nurture it lest they work themselves out of a job and thereby lose their own purpose and identity.

—·—·—·—·—·—·—·—

"In all areas of God's creation He allows His creatures to mature and function on their own. To participate with God in His creation we must, therefore, prepare our children for independence, for that is consistent with His plan."

—·—·—·—·—·—·—·—

Regardless of the motivation or reason for over-protectiveness, we all must realize that sooner or later we will no longer be available to our children. Each generation passes into eternity and upon our death our offspring must be able to get along without us.

The lack of coping skills does not frequently result in a case as extreme as that of Hitchcock's Norman. What we see instead is young people who fumble when they enter adulthood simply because they are ill-equipped to handle the smallest decisions.

For instance, due to lack of exposure to the opposite sex an adolescent girl may fall head-over-heels in love with the first boy who pays any attention to her. Because she has had no experience evaluating a person's character, she cannot see that his attention is purely manipulative. All she knows is that he makes life easy for her. He makes all her decisions about what to do and how to do it, where to go and when, and even what to think.

I observe this frequently in the Christian college setting. Students who have had little exposure to the world and real-life consequences invariably get into trouble the first few weeks of school. Unaccustomed to the relative freedom of a college campus, they sneak off with a group of friends to drink, spend the night at a party, or indulge in some other immature behavior, which, to them, is somehow associated with maturity.

Kids whose parents have let them suffer the consequences of their own behavior before college, who gave them freedom as well as boundaries, don't usually feel the need to express themselves this way. They have seen the folly of such behavior and have grown past it.

There are sometimes more serious results of not teaching teens about consequences. If we don't let them suffer the natural results of their behavior when they are young, while most consequences are relatively minor, reality will teach them when they are older, and by then the consequences may be fatal.

A young woman in a church where I was speaking told me about a boyfriend she had decided to break up with. When she tried to explain to him that she didn't love him and wasn't ready to get married, he pulled a gun out of his pocket and pointed it at his heart. She pleaded with him not to shoot himself, reminding him of all the reasons he had to go on living. But despite all her pleas and arguments, he pulled the trigger and shot himself through the heart. His last words were, "My God, I have killed myself."

This seventeen-year-old boy apparently did not realize until it was too late that the consequence of a bullet through the heart is death.

I don't want to get into a discussion on guns, but I will say that I believe a great percentage of teenage homicides and suicides happen because the young people haven't been taught that actions have consequences.

Although I wish it were otherwise, some young people may never learn certain lessons until they experience the consequences, especially if they've been led to believe there are no consequences or that someone else will always pay them. The cost of certain freedoms is too high to pay for independence, but it's not always possible to convince teenagers of this. Drugs surely fall into that category, as do deviant sexual practices, promiscuity, drunkenness, and the occult. When a young person gets to the place where he or she is actually willing to endure physical harm, there is little a parent can do but back off and let the young person learn the hard way, through cause and effect, as painful as that may be.

———————————

"I believe a great percentage of teenage homicides and suicides happen because

young people haven't been taught that actions have consequences."

It is possible that some teenagers will never be able to hear us speak until their own failures become an embarrassment to them. You may have to wait for your son or daughter to say, "Dad, Mom, I've really screwed things up. Can you help me get my life back together?" When you hear this, or anything similar, that is your signal. You have suddenly become a relevant person and, more important, you have been given a chance to demonstrate the power of God's forgiveness. This goes a long way toward creating an emotionally healthy teenager.

_____ *5* _____

Where Do I Fit?

PRINCIPLE 5

Help your teenager find a niche.

On a paddleboat ride across Lake Geneva in Wisconsin I noticed that one of the high-school kids seemed particularly intent on studying the paddle wheel. I walked up beside him and said, "This is a pretty neat paddle wheel, isn't it?"

"It's not a paddle wheel," he answered.

"Yes it is," I said. "Just look at all the water going around with the paddles."

"Nope," he assured me, "this is a fake paddle wheel."

"Really?" I said. "Tell me about the real ones."

He began to lecture me on Mississippi paddleboats, their history, how many there had been on the river at different times, and what they were used for. It was as if I were talking about Mississippi riverboats with

Mark Twain himself. The boy then told me that the boat we were on was just for tourists and that the paddle wheel was being turned by an electric motor, which didn't make any sense to him at all.

"This paddle wheel's just decoration," he said, and then he explained how the real ones worked. Soon a group of teenagers had gathered around us, listening to all the fascinating things this kid knew about paddleboats.

I learned a very important lesson about teenagers and their needs from this boy. He had found an area of competency. And from it he got his sense of meaning and accomplishment.

Every kid needs to find a niche like this. It might be books, music, woodworking, a collection of some kind, or any number of things, but kids need to find a subject that interests them, one that they can become experts on.

Teenagers don't usually need help in finding a subject that interests them. They know themselves well enough to pick a suitable hobby. But it's at this time when parents need to be especially careful to steer kids toward activities that interest them, not the parents.

For instance, if a father has his heart set on having his son become a shortstop and the son wants to play the cello, the parent would be well advised to let his son be the cello player rather than insist that he get a baseball glove.

This means parents must get their own egos and aspirations under control. It is far more important that we help children find their own area of expertise than that we try to satisfy our own desires for achievement by getting our children to do what we love doing or always wanted to do.

Some men who have been outstanding athletes have sons who have very little interest in sports. One of the reasons, I think, is that they feel they could never compete with their dad. Even if they did well, they wouldn't do as well as he did, and so, not wanting to come in second, they choose something altogether different.

"It is far more important that we help children find their own area of expertise than that we try to satisfy our own desires for achievement by getting our children to do what we love doing or always wanted to do."

The important thing is not finding out what Dad or Mom thinks is important; it's helping young people find something they can do well and enjoy. Young people who find their niche, who do something their parents are proud of, are much more well adjusted than those who can't do anything that pleases anybody.

Fortunately there are groups for just about any kind of special interest imaginable: sports, music, science, art, drama, mathematics, agriculture.

Parents must be prepared, of course, for young people to be fickle, to go from one interest to another. Most junior-high kids have rooms filled with the remains of half-finished or abandoned hobbies. This is all part of searching for and finding a place in life. Parents who are enthusiastic and take an interest in what their kids are interested in will find that their children are more capable of finding the thing they want to do than those who have been discouraged and reprimanded for being so fickle.

Discovering our gifts, abilities, and interests doesn't happen magically as if by special revelation; it comes through trial and error. Sometimes the things we try and set aside, we return to later.

When my son was growing up he got the idea that he wanted to be a magician. Magic was the last thing in the world I was interested in, but Bruce was excited about it. One of the things he wanted was a disappearing box. It was very expensive to buy, but he had gotten the plans somewhere so he talked me into making the box for him. We spent several days in the basement working on this box, making sure the latches and the escape hatch all worked.

Bruce went to school, did his magic act, and then I never heard anything more about it. Several weeks later, I saw the box back in the basement so I asked, "Hey, are you ever going to do that trick again?"

"Nah," he said, "you can only do those tricks once. It wouldn't be a surprise again. Everybody's already seen it."

I had spent hours making the silly box and now he was telling me he was going to do the trick only once. I wanted to say, "Why did we put all that energy into making it for one silly performance?" but I restrained myself. I knew that my grumbling would destroy his enthusiasm for his next idea, and that might be the one that would become his life's work.

Teenagers need to be wholeheartedly sold out to whatever they are doing. The best way for parents to encourage this is to be enthusiastic about the things their kids are enthusiastic about rather than constantly throwing cold water on their ideas. Frankly, this has been one of the more interesting challenges for me as a parent. It is not easy to keep my enthusiasm for ideas I am pretty sure will be short-lived. I have realized, however, that even if I don't believe in the idea, I must believe in my child.

In the religious literature on parenting and child-raising, authors give various interpretations of the Old Testament verse "Train a child in the way he should go, and when he is old he will not turn from it" (Prov. 22:6).

"Parents must be prepared for young people to be fickle, to go from one interest to another. Even if I don't believe in the idea, I must believe in my child."

The interpretation I prefer understands the word *train* in the sense that a gardener would "train" a tree or a sapling. Like a birch tree that bends over a pond, the idea is that we are to train children according to their natural bent and not try to bend them in another direction.

The Bible's most poignant illustration of this point is that of Saul and his son, Jonathan, and the relationship Saul had with Jonathan's best friend, David. The Bible makes it pretty clear that Saul had a love-hate relationship with David. David was the kind of son Saul always wanted. Jonathan didn't quite meet Saul's expectations the way David did, so there was lots of tension in the relationship. The father couldn't forgive his son for not being what he wanted, and the son couldn't do anything to please the father.

Many teens live in this kind of relationship with a parent, and they feel like failures because they can't live up to expectations. Hundreds of kids have told me they just can't be what Dad or Mom wants them to be. And it's usually not because they haven't tried.

Although it is probably impossible to hide our preferences from our children, we would be wise to adapt our interests to theirs rather than try to make them adapt to ours.

A situation at the university last week pointed this out to me. A father and mother brought their daughter up from a southern state to take a look at Taylor University. When I asked why they were interested in having their daughter come to Taylor and what her interest was in the school, the father said, "Well, we are interested in a quality Christian education, and she is interested in your equestrian program."

What a wonderful way for parents to encourage their child, I thought. Although it became clear that neither parent was interested in horses, both were interested in their daughter.

Helping your kids find a niche and then supporting them in it is one of the most important things you can do. Everybody needs a cheerleader, and when kids realize their moms and dads are their cheerleaders, it means a great deal to them.

This year our basketball team went all the way to the final four in the NAIA (National Association of Intercollegiate Athletics) tournament, which is the most successful any of our teams has ever been. Traditionally, the seniors stand up at the annual banquet and tell about their four years under Coach Patterson and what the program has meant to each of them. This year as the boys thanked various people for their contributions to the team, each thanked his parents.

The parents of all three of these senior boys probably had not missed more than five or six games in the four years their sons had played at Taylor. These loyal parents had traveled miles back and forth to watch their boys play. Obviously their interest in and commitment to their sons was very great.

And so I saw these three big young men with four years of college basketball behind them saying, with tears, "Mom, Dad, thank you so much for being interested in me, for believing in me."

At the other extreme, however, was the kid who showed me his picture in the yearbook with all his accomplishments listed beside his name. "You know," he said, "my dad doesn't know one thing about any of this. He has never been to my school. He has never seen me in anything."

— · — · — · — · — · — · —

"The one thing all parents can do for their kids is to believe in them. This belief and confidence can take kids through times of

discouragement when they really want to give up on a task or give in to temptation."

Kids need to know that someone, preferably their parents, supports them. One thing that has confirmed this belief for me is the acknowledgments I read in books by people who have made great accomplishments. Invariably they will say, "I appreciate so and so because he or she always believed in me."

The one thing all parents can do for their teens is to believe in them. This belief and confidence can take kids through times of discouragement when they really want to give up on a task or give in to temptation.

Working with Youth for Christ gave me a good deal of contact with the juvenile justice system when kids got into trouble with the law. I always tried to figure out why certain kids got into trouble. I would see young people in juvenile detention halls stand around all day half dressed, never get cleaned up or comb their hair. They seemed totally defeated and completely devoid of self-respect. I would ask myself, *What is the difference between these kids and the bright-eyed students I meet day after day on high-school and college campuses? Why do some kids go one way and some go the other?*

Societal factors contribute to this, I know, but I believe the biggest difference is the parents.

I have met kids with all kinds of social forces work-ing against them who have achieved things far greater than anyone ever dreamed they could. By and large their achievements have been the result of parents who believed in them and who were their biggest fans. You see it in all walks of life—kids doing things while their parents stand by the sidelines watching, beam-ing, and giving them a nod of encouragement.

Then you see the kids with parents whose words and body language never encourage them to be any-thing but failures. Their chances of survival, much less success, are minimal. Very few people can survive, much less succeed, without someone at their side to encourage them. It is imperative, therefore, that par-ents provide this kind of support for their teenagers because it is unlikely that anyone else will. It is key to growing an emotionally healthy teenager.

6

The Windup
and the Pitch

PRINCIPLE 6

Listen more than you lecture.

*D*elivering effective communication is similar to pitching a baseball game. If a pitcher tries to throw all strikes, the batters will learn what to expect and soon will be knocking balls out of the park. A good pitcher has to throw a few pitches high and inside and a few low and in the dirt to keep the batter guessing.

In communicating with our teenagers we can't expect to throw all strikes in every conversation. It's not even good strategy to try. It doesn't win any baseball games, and it won't grow good kids. Parents who structure communication like a to-do list instead of a game of strategy may get the necessary subjects covered, but neither parent nor child will enjoy the process or get any satisfaction out of it.

Over the years I have asked many young people to tell me about the most influential person in their lives. Very seldom do they mention someone who gave well-formulated philosophical answers based on brilliant, well-developed ideas. Instead, they mention someone who spent time with them, who listened to them, who made them feel important.

If I ask kids about the twenty-five sermons they heard me preach last year, I am surprised if they can reconstruct a single one. But they remember every detail of any personal attention I gave them.

Sometimes a kid will hang around after I speak. At first I assume he's just waiting for a ride, but if everyone else leaves I figure he's waiting for an opportunity to talk. So I will say, "Hey, would you help me carry this stuff to my car?"

On the way out, the kid will usually say, "I didn't want to ask this in front of the other kids, but . . ."

Parents will find the same thing to be true. It is during the informal times, not during structured family forums, that we often have the most meaningful communication with our teenagers.

Communication is more like ketchup than milk. You can't just turn the bottle upside down and have it come out. You've got to wait, prod it a little, and wait some more. Good communication requires a proper mood, a proper setting, careful preparation, good rapport, and good timing.

It is very important for parents to use and savor the impromptu times, the serendipitous moments. Whenever you do something unplanned, unexpected, or out of the ordinary you provide opportunities for your children to let down their guard and bring up subjects they would never feel comfortable discussing in a formal setting.

I was taking a couple of teenagers from church with me on an errand when out of the blue one of them said, "Do you ever feel embarrassed to be a man?"

I said, "What do you mean? What about being a man?"

They looked at each other with sort of an embarrassed look, as if they were already farther into the subject than they wanted to be, and one said, "Well, last night we went to a porno flick."

I knew that they were both sixteen or seventeen and unable to get into an adult theater so I asked, "What was the name of the film?" When they told me I was a little relieved because it was an R-rated film showing at a shopping center near my home.

Then I asked, "What makes you ashamed to be a man?" They then told me how the lead character took advantage of a woman and how cruel he was; interested only in sex, he destroyed her life. The fact that there was some nudity had shocked them as well and they felt guilty.

I then opened the subject of human sexuality; we

talked about being male and female, marriage, and the fact that it was all God's idea. We then discussed the biblical stance on human sexuality, the relationship of Christ to the church—the Bride of Christ, the beauty of marital love, reasons for chastity, males' roles in marriage, and the whole range of biblical teaching on the subject including the relationship between *phileo*, *eros*, and *agape* love. The boys then concluded that only in the Christian context is sex beautiful.

I felt gratified and a little bit proud that they felt free to share so openly and that they saw the context of men in Christ so clearly. These teaching moments cannot be planned or set up, but by being there and spending time with your teens, you will find them happening. I believe the Holy Spirit uses these times beyond our understanding.

"It is during the informal times, not during structured family forums, that we often have the most meaningful communication with our teenagers."

Trips in the car, afternoons at the beach, and Saturday morning breakfasts at the pancake house are marvelous opportunities for real communication. They are not times to tell our kids the things we think they ought to know. They are chances for us to find out what they know, what they think, how they think, why they think it, and what principles guide their lives.

While shopping or listening to the car radio you will hear a word in a song or spoken by teenagers that you don't understand, so you'll ask what it means. Then your child becomes the teacher, the expert, and he or she feels proud of knowing something you don't know, and this develops a bond between you. When you admit you don't know everything, kids are more inclined to admit they don't know everything and to come to you to discuss the real issues that trouble them.

A discussion is always more pleasant than a lecture, so do whatever is necessary to keep yourself from preaching a sermon every time one of your kids says something that sets off your alarm. Resist with all your might the temptation to make value judgments about everything they say. This is difficult advice to follow because parents feel the responsibility to direct their teens and keep them on the "straight and narrow."

Teenagers who make off-the-wall comments usually are not stating their convictions. More frequently they are shaping and testing them. They are throwing ideas in front of us to see how we react. If we react with a sense of horror at everything they say that departs from our "accepted" way of thinking, they get the idea (and probably rightfully so) that we are insecure about our own beliefs and that the only way we know to defend them is through ridicule, sarcasm, or a look that says, "You'll send me to an early grave if you keep saying things like that."

The best way to handle an alarming statement is to dig deeper to find the root of the comment rather than bury it so it never surfaces again. Keep in mind that when the seed of an idea is buried it doesn't die, it germinates.

Teenagers need an atmosphere of freedom to explore ideas without ridicule. They need to know that Mom and Dad will give every idea a hearing, respect their opinions, and not put them on trial for heresy for questioning some of their parents' most basic and treasured beliefs.

"When you admit you don't know everything, kids are more inclined to admit they don't know everything and to come to you to discuss the real issues that trouble them."

Most young people suspect, if they don't already know, that there aren't answers to every question. What they are really concerned about is how people cope with unanswered questions, how they balance the contradictions of life. It is the way we live, not what we say, that provides the deepest, most lasting, and most trustworthy answers.

People who don't spend much time with teenagers are unaware of how many serious conversations they have. Teenagers talk about deep philosophical issues. They are interested in creation, in eternity, in the whole subject of the spirit world. And they talk about these things without any prompting from adults.

If parents can learn to be comfortable with their teenagers' tentative ideas, the teenagers will be a lot more willing to talk, and through talking, parents can influence the belief system their kids are formulating.

It is helpful to talk to kids about nonthreatening things to get them used to talking so that when threatening things come along, the lines of communication are already open. For example, sometimes I ask questions about things I have read. I'll look up from the newspaper and say, "It says here that six out of ten teenagers drink beer at least once a week. Why do you think there's so much drinking going on among teenagers?" When they tell me why all the kids are drinking, I find out as much about my own kids as I do about everyone else's.

Or if I'm working on a speech or an article, I'll ask, "If I were to say this to a bunch of kids, what do you think they would say about me?" This gives them the opportunity to tell me their opinion of what other kids think, which, of course, really gives me insight into what they are thinking.

The same technique can be effective when watching the news or even a sitcom on television. You can ask, "What do you think would happen in our family if we did that?" or "How do you think your friend's dad would respond if that happened in their house?" or "How would you solve this problem?" Expressing their views and opinions is good mental exercise for them and insightful for you.

Of course, teenagers know less than adults. If they don't, something is wrong with the adults. So there is no reason for adults to play king of the hill to prove their superiority. However, there is at least one subject that teenagers know infinitely more about than their parents. That subject is themselves. The only things you'll ever know for sure about your kids are the things you let them teach you. It is imperative, therefore, that we are smart enough to listen without lecturing so teenagers feel comfortable talking to us.

Give me five minutes with any teenager and I can tell you if he or she has listening parents or lecturing parents. Teenagers whose parents listen to them, talk to them, and value their opinions are confident, secure, and well adjusted. Teens whose parents lecture them, put them down, finish their sentences, play king of the hill of knowledge, never take their ideas seriously, and always force them into predictable, orthodox responses are unsure of themselves, quiet, and afraid to express opinions.

One of the most important steps in developing independence in kids is to teach them to express themselves clearly, to develop an argument that leads to a logical conclusion, and to be able to defend their opinions yet respect those who hold different ones.

In our family, reading is one of the tools we have used to generate communication.

"One of the most important steps in developing independence in kids is to teach them to express themselves clearly, to develop an argument that leads to a logical conclusion, and to be able to defend their opinions yet respect those who hold different ones."

I find it encouraging that thousands of teenagers and college students today are wearing bracelets with the letters *WWJD* on them. These, of course, are a reminder of a novel called *In His Steps*, written by Charles Sheldon in 1896. The story is simple, dated, and some feel, naive, but I've felt a responsibility to use Sheldon's idea in messages to young people now for more than forty years. Prior to this current interest

I challenged the students in Taylor University chapel to use the question "What would Jesus do?" in every situation they faced over the summer months and then to write me about how it affected their lives.

When I gave the challenge I was aware that most mature adult Christians monitor their daily decisions and relationships with some version of the idea in an almost unconscious way every day; however, it was nothing short of amazing to me how profoundly the question affected the students. I got dozens of carefully written notes, letters, and journal entries covering literally everything from the most ordinary issue to the most difficult ethical and moral dilemmas. To be honest, when I presented the challenge I was almost embarrassed because I feel so deeply the generational chasm between me and the students, yet in their responses I felt our shared humanity and the universal nature of life in Christ.

A book that I read fifty years ago had impact because I dared to share it. As adults and parents we need to take the risk and the time to share our common life together with our children—never more than when they're teens.

Because of his love for the out-of-doors and wildlife, my son got interested in the writings of Jack London. His books and stories got us into great discussions about the cruelty and beauty of nature, the concept of courage, man's relationship to animals and creation, and man's place in the world. As a result, we share a love for nature that will bind us together for a lifetime.

My oldest daughter and I have enjoyed reading the tales of King Arthur and the Knights of the Round Table. *The Once and Future King* has been a starting point for hundreds of meaningful conversations. You can't read about Arthur and his relationship with Lancelot and Guenivere without gaining insights about love, romance, loyalty, fidelity, disappointment, and heartache. These are great issues for fathers and daughters to discuss, and I can't think of anything other than literature that would have given us this opportunity.

More recently we have read George MacDonald's nineteenth-century novels. Based on Christian themes, these stories generate better discussions about theology than any sermons I've ever heard.

When our children were young, verbal communication was limited pretty much to the do's and don'ts of life. As the children matured, our discussions moved to a higher plane, that of who, what, and when. And then came one of the greatest joys of being a parent. Finally we reached the highest plane of communication with our children, the why level. The transition to conversations with emotionally healthy teens about ideas, values, and philosophies is a marvelous and rewarding adventure. Be sure you don't miss it.

7

Send in the Clowns

Principle 7

Look on the funny side of life.

Shortly after I got my driver's license I was driving too close to the middle of a narrow road and I sideswiped another car. The crash tore the front fender, two doors, and the rear fender from my dad's car. After I found out everyone was okay, I stood in the ditch and prayed, "Dear God, I pray this didn't happen." I opened my eyes and saw that the car was still wrecked, so I closed my eyes, squinted real hard, and prayed again, "Dear God, it didn't happen." Then I opened my eyes, but it happened anyway.

My son loves this story. It gives him great pleasure to know that I messed up in such a big way, and it tickles him that his old pious pa didn't even have the sense to pray a sensible prayer.

Though it is hard for parents to believe, our children do look up to us. We know all the problems and failures we had growing up and that we are just ordinary people. But most of us have done a pretty good job of hiding that knowledge from our kids. We sugarcoat our past with phrases like "When I was a kid, I never spoke to my parents like that."

As a result, our kids grow up feeling inferior to us. They tend to feel that we have turned out perfect and that any failure on their part makes it impossible for them to ever grow up right and become like us.

For this reason, it is very helpful for parents to have the sense of security that allows them to make fun of themselves, their struggles trying to fit in, and their failures. When kids struggle with failure and less-than-satisfactory accomplishments, it is of great value to be able to tell them about the times we failed and, above all, to laugh about them.

As a youth worker and communicator, I have learned to use a technique I call "leading from weakness." A long time ago I realized that very few struggling people can identify with someone who does everything easily and well or who always ends up the hero of his own stories. I am a much more effective communicator when I identify with the weakest and then show the struggle from weakness to accomplishment. Therefore, in virtually all the stories I tell about myself or my family, we are the brunt of the joke. That is, we have had a struggle or a problem and as a result have gleaned some insight that others can use.

This is a technique that can be extremely helpful in parenting. Most of us are weak and have a great deal of failure in our lives, so when kids I know try and fail, I remind them of the times I too have tried and failed.

One of our kids found a Bible of mine that had "J. K. plus A. A." written on the edge of the pages, and my tale of woe about Amy Acton became a favorite family story. Amy Acton was a little girl I adored with all my heart from third through eighth grades. But Amy was unattainable for me. In fact, she ended up marrying a neighbor who was always bigger and stronger and who always won everything. I could never compete with him in anything, so it was no surprise that I lost Amy to him.

The Amy Acton story came in handy whenever one of our teens was struggling with puppy love. Every time one of them got hurt by a boyfriend or girlfriend I would retell the story about the unattainable young girl I thought about every minute, even though she wouldn't give me the time of day. Eventually they realized that people can survive rejection and heartbreak and even go on to find happiness with someone else.

"Humor lets off some of the steam in the pressure cooker in which young people live."

Most kids develop a crush on someone who is unattainable and it is good for them to know that this is not abnormal, that one day they will meet someone even more special, and that they will look back on this experience as humorous.

Humor lets off some of the steam in the pressure cooker in which young people live. The person who has developed this kind of humor into an art form is Bill Cosby. Realizing that his experiences growing up are pretty much universal, he has turned them into stories that connect with most of the American population. He finds the humor in every situation.

Many of the difficult experiences of growing up are universal. The inability to get a good grade from a particular teacher. The lack of talent to make the basketball team. The feeling that you are not coordinated enough to be a cheerleader. Being rejected by the particular boy or girl you have a crush on. The feeling that you aren't smart enough to get into college. The fear that you are ugly, that your body is not developing properly, that you are too skinny, too fat, too flat-chested, too voluptuous.

These types of insecurities are common to everyone who has ever been a teenager. Your teenagers need to know that you and every other adult they know have survived these problems that seem insurmountable and life-threatening to them now. This is a delicate balance. You don't want to trivialize the problems by saying they are unimportant, but you do want to give them perspective by showing the humorous side.

We mentioned earlier the role of the family album in showing our children's developmental process and giving us insights into their needs and struggles for independence. It is also useful to get out the family album from our generation and let the kids see pictures of us when we were young. When they see our knobby knees and strange clothes, they will get a better perspective of how things change over time. They will see that how people look as children bears little resemblance to how they look as adults.

This tends to give kids a sense of confidence and assurance that everything will turn out well. If the funny-looking little girl with the knobby knees and skinny arms climbing a tree in the backyard can become the mother they adore and respect, maybe they too will turn out all right.

Humor that involves ourselves helps to accomplish this goal. Humor that goes the other way is much more difficult. In fact, when the other person is the brunt of the humor, it requires a much greater understanding and sensitivity.

_._._._._._._._._

"Kidding and joshing can lighten up many family situations, but when kidding turns into teasing that sends a child crying from the room feeling frustrated and demeaned, humor has been misused."

_._._._._._._._._

I am a very strong advocate of humor that goes both ways. Kidding and joshing can lighten up many family situations. However, many people are unable to keep it balanced, and they are best advised to back off and not try humor in their relationships with kids.

When kidding turns into teasing that sends a child crying from the room feeling frustrated and demeaned, humor has been misused. In fact, that is not humor at all.

I have observed this in many youth workers over the years and have tried to help them understand this subtle difference. With just a little bit of sensitivity an adult can quickly learn to determine whether the young person is joining in and enjoying the teasing or is being hurt by it because the problem is too deep or too serious to be treated frivolously.

One of the most rewarding relationships I have

enjoyed has been with my youngest daughter. I think it got started because a family friend spoke such endearing words about his daughter that it got to be funny to us. He was always bragging about her, saying how pretty she was, how neat she was, and so on. He even referred to her as "Princess" in public. It eventually got to the point that our kids were embarrassed for his daughter.

So I began calling Terri "Buzzard Bait" whenever the friend called his daughter "Princess." Terri got a kick out of this because it was our private joke. She knew that I loved her and adored her but would never embarrass her by calling her "Princess" in public.

This good-natured teasing gave us a lot of laughs and contributed to our closeness all through her college years and until her marriage. In fact, even today she will occasionally say to me, "It's no wonder I turned out so bad, you called me 'Buzzard Bait' and he called her 'Princess.'"

However, if I had ever once sensed that my teasing was hurting her in any way, I would have stopped immediately. And I would very strongly advise parents that if there is any doubt about your ability to tease good-naturedly, stick to humor that makes you the brunt of the joke.

Teasing is subtle and can cut very deeply into a fragile ego. It should never, ever be used to "toughen up" a child you think is too sensitive. A child with fragile self-esteem can be destroyed by insensitive teasing. But humor at the parent's expense is generally safe and will lighten many situations that seem grim and unsolvable to a teenager.

One of the most difficult things for teenagers to grasp is that life will turn out all right. They tend to see each situation as an end in itself. But if they get the sense that Mom and Dad have lived through the same things and now look back on them and laugh, they will realize that they will be able to do the same thing some day.

Being in public ministry, I have done lots of things that have given my family opportunities to make jokes at my expense. Several years ago I was invited to speak at my daughter's high-school commencement. I was honored, of course, because she was graduating from a large, public high school and I knew the superintendent must have had a lot of confidence in me, a religious leader, to trust me to speak at such an important event.

— — · — · — · — · — · — · — —

"When parents can laugh at themselves, teenagers learn that ridicule or criticism is not a life-and-death matter."

— — · — · — · — · — · — · — —

However, knowing that kids are very sensitive about all the things parents can do to embarrass them, I was also concerned that I not do or say anything that would mortify my daughter on this special day in her life. So I prepared very carefully, going over and over my speech to make sure nothing in it would cause her any embarrassment.

On commencement day, the graduates accepted their diplomas, moved their tassels, and I made my speech. When it was over, I left feeling quite proud of myself for not making any boo-boos.

After we got home, however, Janie burst my bubble by describing what had gone on in the audience. During my address a teenager behind her began to get very restless. His mother kept telling him to be quiet, but he would just sigh loudly and shift noisily in his folding chair. Finally he asked, "Mom, when is Old Motormouth going to quit?"

When Janie told this story we all laughed like mad because our kids had behaved that way when listening to other speakers, and now old Dad was in the same category as those other "motormouths."

Hearing me laugh about it and realizing that my self-esteem stayed intact even though some kid had insulted me seemed to give my daughter a great sense of relief. When parents can laugh at themselves, teenagers learn that ridicule or criticism is not a life-and-death matter.

Whenever people are in the public eye they will be criticized, and it's important for kids to realize this.

If they can understand that the voice of criticism is not the voice of authority, they will realize that there is no need to get angry or defensive about every barb or insult.

Humor is imperative in parenting emotionally healthy teenagers. If you don't learn how to laugh, you'll shed a lot of unnecessary tears.

— 8 —

Do As I Do

PRINCIPLE 8

Let your teenagers see how you love and obey Christ.

When I was a kid, my dad did all sorts of things that I considered truly amazing. If a cow got outside the fence, Dad would tell me how the animal would behave and how I should get behind it, turn its head, and start it going the other way. Dad could neuter a pig, find a mother chicken and her nest, and tighten the top wire on a fence so it would sound like a violin or a piano. He did a thousand things around the house and farm that made me think he could do anything. In fact, I used to brag all the time about what my dad could do.

I seldom meet young men today who feel this way

about their fathers. In fact, most young people have no opportunity to see their parents at work, to see how much they know or what they are able to do. A century ago, sons learned from their fathers and daughters learned from their mothers. But now there are so many new occupations and technologies that parents are often unable to give specific counsel about the world their children are going to face. We would like to be able to mentor our children, to have them follow the path we have chosen, but this is seldom possible today.

So rather than suggest that Christians spend their time reading magazines about country life and trying to re-create the good old days when children worked beside their parents and learned from them, it would be more valuable to look at what we as modern parents can teach our children other than an occupation. "Do as I do" is still a good concept, but there is a way to look at it other than vocationally.

Satisfaction Guaranteed

The Bible speaks of love, joy, peace, long-suffering, gentleness, goodness, faith, meekness, and temperance as being the "fruit of the Spirit." These are qualities of life that are guaranteed to make us pleasing to God and at the same time, successful and useful in the world in which we live, regardless of where we live or what we do.

These characteristics assure success and happiness regardless of vocational preference. Parents who can demonstrate these qualities will encourage their teens to develop them in the same way that parents of previous generations taught specific tasks. And parents who can teach their children these virtues pass on something of much greater value than the knowledge of how to string a fence or outwit a wayward cow.

The question then becomes: "How do we teach these qualities to our children?"

"Rather than spend our time reading magazines about country life and trying to re-create the good old days when children worked beside their parents, it would be more valuable to look at what modern parents can teach their children other than an occupation."

There is no substitute for the kind of side-by-side human contact between parent and child that the earlier, "simpler" life demanded just because most chores required more than one person. In the modern world, where the father gets on a commuter train and goes into the city to work in an impersonal, international corporation, the son finds it difficult to understand what it is that swallows up his father, saps his energy, and sends him home too exhausted to be much fun. That father, rather than spending his Saturday showing his son where he works, should probably choose something that involves more interaction. It could be golfing, fishing, yard work, repairing the house, going to church for a workday, or a lot of different things. The important thing is for the son to see the father in the context of a real-world situation and to see how the father reacts in that environment.

A family I know has a cottage at a lake in northern Wisconsin. When they arrived there one spring Saturday, they discovered that their dock had been torn loose by a storm and was all the way across the lake wedged against the shore. The father and son discussed the problem. How were they going to get their dock back?

They decided that towing it with their boat would be dangerous, and perhaps illegal, so they put on their swimming trunks, swam across the very cold, very large lake, and swam back home, pulling the dock behind them.

The father was the first to tell me about this experience, which he described as exhausting, exasperating, and miserable.

Later I mentioned it to the son. "Say," I said, "I heard you and your dad had an interesting experience Saturday with the dock."

"Yeah," he said, "we sure did." Then he began to tell me how heavy the dock was and how difficult it was to pull, and then he began to describe his dad's tenaciousness. "I didn't know Dad could do that. He really hung in there. I was ready to quit, but Dad just kept pulling. I would have given up, but you know my dad, he won't give up on anything. We stayed at it and stayed at it. That was about the best time Dad and I ever had together. We did everything but cuss at the thing, but we eventually got it across. And we did it all by ourselves. We didn't have to call anybody to do it or anything. I tell you, I am going to appreciate that dock a whole lot more now that I've had to drag it clear across the lake."

That boy learned something important about his dad and what makes him successful. The truth of the matter is that the boy's father is a very successful businessman who has provided a beautiful lake cottage for his family. But it hasn't happened without effort. He is an extremely tenacious person who, over the last fifteen years, has gone through a couple of severe financial crises that might have broken the spirits of other men. But he has stuck with it and has come out on the other side. Now the son understands that the reason his dad is successful is not because favorable things just happen to him; his dad is successful because he keeps on swimming no matter how cold or hot the water.

This is a tremendous lesson for young people to learn in a world where so many people take short-cuts, believing that success comes through conniving, shaving corners, or manipulating people or rules. This boy may never again have to swim across a lake with a raft in tow, but he will be called on a thousand times in the future to stick with a task and see it to its end.

"The fidelity of our love for one another, our family, friends, church, pastor, and those around us will transfer to our kids, who will, by our example, learn to love deeply, be loyal, and exhibit fidelity in everything they do."

Another friend of mine was an extremely dependent woman before her husband died several years ago. She relied on him to provide all the good things in life and to make virtually all family decisions. His death left her with three children and a tremendous amount of responsibility. Rather than sit and wring her hands, she decided to go back to school and gain some professional abilities so she could run the family business. Over the course of several years, she earned her degree and in so doing gained the confidence to carry on the business, which she now operates very successfully.

Her daughter, having watched her mother, has become actively involved in the business as well. This mother has provided an example that will be of great benefit to her daughter as she faces the problems, setbacks, and discouragements bound to come her way.

These two stories illustrate that the change in the work world and the advancement of technology do not mean that today's parents have nothing to offer their teenagers that will contribute to their future success.

The important stuff we pass on is the material from which our teenagers' futures will be made. And it is closely related to the fruit of the Spirit. The fidelity of our love for one another, our family, friends, church, pastor, and those around us, will transfer to our kids, who will, by our example, learn to love deeply, be loyal, and exhibit fidelity in everything they do. They will observe and learn from the way we overcome obstacles and difficulties.

When I meet young people who believe that everyone is against them and are filled with bitterness, anger, and resentment, I usually find that their parents have the same view of life. Unable to accept personal responsibility for their actions, they have shifted responsibility to others, concluding that their difficulties are the result of someone else's selfish ways.

This martyr complex, characterized by whining, complaining, and blaming others, filters down to their children, causing them the same sort of heartaches that the parents have had.

Another way young people become like their parents is in the subtle area of values. They learn something new from us every day and will live their lives according to the models we give them to follow. So the question we must ask ourselves is, *How can I perform in a competent, mature manner so that when my kids copy me, I will be happy with what I observe in them?*

There are two very basic components that maximize the impact we can have on our kids' lives as they imitate our behavior.

—·—·—·—·—·—·—

"The question we must ask ourselves is, How can I perform in a competent, mature manner so that when my kids copy me, I will be happy with what I observe in them?"

—·—·—·—·—·—·—

First, we must believe in the values we live by. If we are not convinced that our values have worth, no amount of lecturing, arguing, or rule setting will get the point across. In fact, if we choose this method, our children will learn more about lecturing, arguing, and setting rules than they learn about making moral choices and living godly lives. Through the study of God's Word, commitment to Christ, fellowship with other believers, and responsible living we will gain faith in the biblical building material we are using.

A friend of mine went to school in the early days of the Ford Motor Company's engineering institute and wound up in a high position in the automobile industry. He tells of a German professor who used to say to the young men, "Have faith in steel."

My friend, though he is nearly eighty years old now, vividly remembers the professor who forcefully pronounced steel the most reliable building material for automobiles. You could have faith in a car built of steel, he preached. It would hold up under the tremendous temperature extremes and the great stresses and strains that are put on an automobile over hundreds of thousands of miles.

The steel needed to build teenagers of strong character comes from the principles of God's Word. Family living based on these guidelines will enable us to produce young adults who will not fall apart after a few miles of wear and tear.

"The one who is in you is greater than the one who is in the world," wrote John in his first epistle (4:4). Many Christians I meet seem to doubt this, however. They act as if the Christian faith is some kind of flimsy, poorly constructed vehicle that falls to pieces at every little bump in the road. Not so. The Christian faith is made of solid stuff. It's stronger than any metal turned out in a Pittsburgh steelyard. God made us and has given us instructions which, when followed, guarantee that we will hold up despite the wear and tear on our lives.

Our kids may run into situations where the principles don't seem to work. They will see kids in school who cheat and get ahead. But still we keep living, modeling, and teaching the principle of honesty. I have always said to our kids, "You stick by the principles, you do as God has told us to do, and let God take care of the consequences. Even if a teacher isn't smart enough to understand what has happened and you get a lower grade because the curve has been raised by one or two cheaters, be honest. Honesty is more important than the grade. If that happens, God knows, you know, I know, and the family knows what happened, and we are just as proud of you as if you had gotten an A+ because you got it God's way, the honest way."

"God made us and has given us instructions which, when followed, guarantee that we will hold up despite the wear and tear on our lives."

It has been a great source of joy for Janie and me to watch our kids continue with some of the convictions we lived by when they were young. For instance, we have always believed and taught that if we tithe our income, God will bless the remaining nine-tenths and make it worth more than ten-tenths when it comes time to pay the bills. Now we hear our children talk about "God's money." The tithe belongs to God, not to them, and although their gross income is relatively small, a percentage of it always goes to the Lord's work—some missionary enterprise, church building project, needy neighbor, or a practical gift of charity. As I look at what they have, I believe God is blessing them because they are living by principles that glorify Him.

Second, we must live by the values we believe in. "Like father, like son" is a phrase all of us have heard. As a college president I get to know many young people, and when I get to meet their parents I am amazed at the likenesses. I often notice that temperament traits required for certain kinds of careers are passed from parent to child. The son of an engineer father who pays scrupulous attention to detail will likely approach tasks in the same manner. The salesman father who is interested in relationships and can create harmony between individuals somehow passes these skills on to his son.

We could get into a debate as to whether these traits are genetic or learned, but I think the argument would be largely academic. The truth of the matter is, we have a very powerful tool available to us in the parenting process, and that tool is our own lives. Therefore, the emphasis of the wise parent is on personal competence, not on perfecting the son's or daughter's behavior.

Our teenagers will learn from watching us, so all the harping and nagging we do about their behavior is less effective than steady, consistent modeling of the behavior we want to see in them.

I reject the idea that modern parents are helpless. Sometimes when we hear about new discoveries in science and math or that there are forty thousand occupations that did not exist when we were going to school, we feel as if we have nothing to offer our young people. We long for the days when life was simpler.

Well, life is not going to get simpler. In fact, it's probably going to get more complex. But the things that are important never change. God is the same yesterday, today, and forever, and the things we alone can teach our children—godly values—will never change or be outdated.

Faith Is Caught, Not Taught

Through watching parents relate to their heavenly Father, children learn how to relate to their earthly father. They also submit to parents as they see their parents submit to God.

There is a great deal of difference between a

religious home and a Christian home. A religious home is filled with rules, regulations, and a lot of ritual. Much of what goes on in these homes has more to do with traditions and preferences than with godly living.

"The emphasis of the wise parent is on personal competence, not on perfecting the son's or daughter's behavior."

A Christian home is one where faith permeates the lives of the parents and is a natural part of all their decision making. The family's values are as vital to them as the air they breathe, the water they drink, and the food they eat. Values are just as important in the daily activities of work and play as they are in moments of crucial decisions.

It is important for teenagers to understand each parent's pilgrimage of faith. Tell them about your religious thought life, your path to faith, your own conversion experience, how you have grown spiritually, your doubts and questions, and how you have come to certain conclusions about faith and life style. Why do you attend a particular church? Why have you accepted a certain theology? What does your faith mean to you at work? Who is on your prayer list? What are the concerns you have about world missions?

In short, our children need to understand what makes us tick spiritually. Once they understand our journey of faith they will better understand why we do certain things and make certain choices. Being stuck with a couple of parents who are religious for no apparent reason can totally destroy a child's faith.

Hundreds of times each week parents get an opportunity to express the way their faith affects daily living. A family prayer time, whether before meals or before bed, is surely one of those opportunities. If we are careful not to allow these daily worship opportunities to become perfunctory, they will help us communicate to our kids the vital role God plays in our lives. We pray for those who are sick, in financial need, have lost a loved one to death, are facing a difficult decision, or are considering a major purchase or move. All of these things become a part of the spiritual diet of our kids day by day.

No prayer has greater meaning than the one that says, "Your will be done on earth as it is in heaven." As we consign into the hands of a loving, all-powerful, all-knowing, all-compassionate God, our kids get a sense that it is indeed Christ who gives us meaning and purpose. Even as we experience catastrophe and disappointment, they see in our words and attitudes the belief that "His ways are above our ways."

Let's face it, we pray for a great many people who do not get better. Loved ones die. Will our young people see parents who feel as if God has let them down, or parents who trust God's judgment and accept the outcome whether it goes with or against their desires? The latter tells them that we trust the heavenly Father more than our own desires and judgments.

In fact, it is in losses that some of the greatest lessons are taught. As we stand with our children beside the casket of a loved one, we can show them how to embrace both grief and hope and find peace. As members of the family of God console one another, children learn that they are part of a bigger family and that we all are in God's hands.

A Spiritual Laboratory

Family life is a kind of spiritual laboratory. The ingredients of everyday experiences are poured into the test tube of life, which, if we are believers, is already filled with God.

Then we watch the results as God carries out His will in front of us. There should be an observable difference between the reaction of ingredients coming into a life filled with God and that of ingredients coming into a life void of God. If children see no difference between the way their believing parents handle problems and the way the unbelieving parents of their friends handle similar situations, they will probably question their parents' faith, and with good reason.

"Being stuck with a couple of parents who are religious for no apparent reason can totally destroy a child's faith."

Our children's experiences give meaning to the words they hear in church and Sunday school. Sermons and lessons have meaning only as they relate to the experiences that have shaped our understanding of the words used. If kids have heard about love but have never been loved, they don't understand love. If they have heard about compassion but have never felt it or seen it in action, they don't understand compassion. If they have heard about patience but have never been recipients of it, they will have a problem understanding the patience of God.

Virtually all spiritual lessons come from living with one another, especially with parents. In one sense, the entire relationship parents have with children is a process of Christian education. This is what the book of Deuteronomy means when it talks about wearing truths on our sleeve and on our forehead and having them written on the doorposts of our house. It is not talking about some kind of giant graffiti display where

Bible verses are written all over the walls. It is talking about parents who raise children in an atmosphere permeated with the influence of God, where trusting God is as natural as breathing.

Living as a citizen of the kingdom of God is similar to living as a citizen of the United States. We learn the laws of the land and understand the rights and responsibilities of being a citizen by living here and having the culture permeate our being. Not many kids have ever seen the president of the United States in person, and the majority have not visited Washington, D.C., yet they know what it means to be an American because they are surrounded by other Americans. Teenagers learn what it means to be a citizen of the kingdom of God by living with us and seeing how we relate to God.

Unfortunately, no parent will ever be the perfect example of Christianity. But fortunately, our failures, when handled properly, can be as effective a teaching tool as our successes. As teens watch us process disappointment and personal failure without attempting to rationalize or avoid responsibility, they learn to handle their own failures in a forthright manner.

I have had many opportunities to observe kids whose parents have gotten into deep trouble. One father was sent to prison for embezzlement and one mother got caught in an adulterous relationship. Whether or not this became a positive spiritual lesson for the child depended on how the parent handled it. It has been amazing for me to see how well kids can handle the failure of a parent and how much they mature spiritually if the mother or father is forthright about it. If a parent says, "I have sinned. I did wrong. Please forgive me," almost without exception their children are able to do that. When children are allowed to deal with failure as mature young adults, they are usually able to handle it successfully and grow spiritually through the experience.

"If children see no difference between the way their believing parents handle problems and the way the unbelieving parents of their friends handle similar situations, they will probably question their parents' faith, and with good reason."

However, if parents refuse to acknowledge their wrongdoing and try to deceive their children by lying, misleading, or covering up the sin, usually the child begins a spiritual decline. Resentment often sets in, and the disillusioned child begins a long journey through a spiritual desert.

The Christian faith is not just about success; it is also about how we handle disappointment, failure, and our own humanity. It shows us how to live honestly and forthrightly. And it shows us that the only way to deal with failure is to allow the strong arms of God to embrace us and redeem us.

Parents who are patient with the failures of their young people tend to receive greater patience from their children. Parents who are obedient to God make it easier for their teens to obey parents and God as well. Parents who are transparent, vulnerable, and open find that their teenagers tend to develop these same qualities in relationships, not only with God but with them as well.

If I were asked to name the single greatest fault of parents, I would say that it is their unwillingness to be genuine. Perhaps many parents fear that if they allow their kids to see that they have any spiritual struggles, the kids will lose faith in them, and thus the parents will lose their spiritual authority. Quite the opposite is true. Kids know, especially as they enter the teenage years, that parents are subject to all the weaknesses and failures of humanity. What they cannot stand is hypocrisy. They will not tolerate deception, and when they see it, they feel obligated to break through and reveal the person for what he or she truly is. In fact, many young people get into trouble in their own lives in an attempt to prove that "at least I'm not a hypocrite."

If parents would be willing to tell their kids about their own spiritual struggles and victories, they would help their kids reach a much higher level of spiritual development than by pretending they are capable of some form of spiritual perfection.

What's the Attraction?

Kids are not attracted to perfection; they are attracted to authenticity and genuineness. If we ask their help, seek their prayers, and welcome their advice when we are struggling with various problems, they will be more tolerant, more responsible, and more respectful than if we pretend Christianity is a breeze and that we're out waving in it like a flag.

If parents would replace the word *perfect* with *authentic*, their ability to guide and encourage the spiritual growth of their children would be enhanced immeasurably.

"If I were asked to name the single greatest fault of parents, I would say that it is their unwillingness to be genuine."

Don't be afraid to share the details of your Christian life with your teenagers, for that is how they learn to live it. As you imitate Christ, they imitate you. This is the biblical pattern of Christian growth.

Recently a father told me about a phone call he'd gotten from his son.

"Dad," the son said, "I've watched your Christian life all these years, but I've been a long way from being the kind of man you wanted me to be. But tonight I'm calling to tell you that all your prayers and good living have paid off. I just got on my knees and recommitted my life to Christ, and I wanted you to be the first to know."

That father started crying all over again when he told me that story. Sometimes we have to wait a long time for our kids to come full circle, to reach emotional health. But God has had to wait a long time for many of us, so we're in good company.

What About Rebellion?

PRINCIPLE 9

Stay calm; it's seldom as serious as you think.

When our son, Bruce, was a freshman in high school, young people were putting a great deal of emphasis on hair. In fact, the Broadway play *Hair* was popular then and kids across the nation were growing Afros. In one of Bruce's pictures his hair comes straight out from his head for a full three inches. You've never seen so much hair with such a small face peeking out of it, except maybe on a baby orangutan. Although the whole family sees it as hilarious now, it was a serious matter back then.

Bruce was going through a stage in which it was very difficult for him to be the son of a preacher and religious leader. He had to prove to others that he had his own identity, that he was more than just his father's son. And so, without doing anything mean or hurtful, he made a quiet statement with his hair. It became a symbol of his independence.

For some time I rode his back quite heavily about his haircut (or lack thereof). But one night when my mother was visiting she helped me get things back in perspective.

"Jay," she said, "don't you remember when your sister was getting ready to graduate from high school and you came home that night with a buzz haircut? It was so short it looked like your head had been shaved. I was so embarrassed and angry I couldn't think of any punishment serious enough, short of murder. You went upstairs for a few minutes and came back to the table with a sack over your head with holes cut in it for the eyes and a mouth. You took away all my anger by making me laugh as you tried to eat from underneath the grocery sack.

"Come on now, Jay, it isn't that big of a deal, is it?"

Mother's comments made me realize that my concern about my son's hair had more to do with my own self-esteem and my concern about what my friends would think of me for allowing my son to wear his hair that way than it had to do with my concern for his well-being. After a good laugh we decided that hair length wasn't going to change the course of the world, or even the course of our family life unless I continued to make an issue of it.

Much of what gets labeled as rebellion in teenagers really isn't that at all. More frequently it's part of the natural struggle for an independent identity.

Through aspects of popular culture like fashion and music, teenagers say, "We want a world that is ours, where we set the rules, where we can run our lives without interference."

This is not a new teenage phenomenon, and within certain bounds it is desirable. We want our children to develop an identity apart from ours, but we're not always good at helping them acquire it.

Walls Won't Work

Parents live somewhere between two realities: that of knowing the dangers of independence (knowing them so well, in fact, that they terrify us) and knowing that we cannot protect our young people. Kids will, if they desire, find the opportunity and the ingenuity to break our rules and violate our will.

"Much of what gets labeled as rebellion in teenagers really isn't that at all. More frequently it's part of the natural struggle for an independent identity."

Knowledge of these possibilities causes many parents to try building walls around their young people with words, warnings, even threats. Rather than provide protection, though, these walls create divisions, which nearly guarantee that our kids will get into deep trouble.

Our Motive Is Love

Teenagers particularly must continually be assured that we love them and are trying to protect them. Even though we may sometimes be unable to communicate it, our motive must always be love. When young people have this assurance they are more likely to give us the benefit of the doubt—even when they don't totally understand our reasons for certain restrictions.

I don't accept the fact that rebellion is a natural stage of growing up. Yes, the Bible tells of many young people who disobeyed their parents and whose behavior ended in devastating tragedies, but God never spoke of such rebellion as an inevitable part of growing up. In fact, He always warned against it.

The parenting task demands that we set up guidelines for children while they are very young. We must make our expectations clear and make sure they understand what happens if they overstep the established bounds. As early as possible and as often as possible, give reasons for your boundaries.

Parents who are able to affirm good behavior, reward good intentions and accomplishments, yet understand failures and offer forgiveness, will usually have teenagers who trust them and follow their advice.

We Speak from Experience

As kids grow older, parents can share more and more insights from their own lives and tell the lessons they've learned from various experiences, both good and bad. Let's face it, we want our children to know everything we know without ever having to go through the difficult experiences we've had along the way. It would indeed be wonderful if kids could learn vicariously from our experiences. And they can, within limits, but only if we're honest about them. Parents tend to speak in vague generalities about their less-than-honorable teenage exploits because they don't want to give their kids any more ideas than they already have.

But the more honest you can be about your mistakes and what you learned from them, the more credibility you'll have with your kids.

Trust God to Provide Protection

Parents cannot hover over their children like an invisible guardian angel, but God can. He sees our kids when they go off with friends who seem a little flaky. And He has witnessed all our efforts to raise them and instruct them according to the principles He has given.

I believe He rewards parental faithfulness by building the protective wall around our children that we are unable to build, thereby keeping them from the heartaches they might experience if they were not the object of a loving parent's prayer.

"We do more than react to the evil in the world; we work alongside God to eradicate it."

God has made us of good stuff. Not only can we survive in a hostile world, we can thrive in it and even improve it as we participate with God in His redemptive plan. We do more than react to the evil in the world; we work alongside God to eradicate it.

Is It Rebellion or Ignorance?

Two other motives for teenage behavior that frequently get mislabeled as rebellion are ignorance and curiosity.

A father called me one day for advice concerning a situation with his son. He had heard noise in the house at about 12:30 the previous morning. When he got up to check on it, he discovered his son coming in from a night out with friends. As they walked toward each other, the son staggered and fell against the wall. Though angry that his son was drunk, the father realized he was also going to be very sick from so much alcohol, so he kept his temper under control and helped his son into bed. The next morning he called me to ask what he should do.

My advice was brief. "Find out what happened," I said. "Before you do anything, listen to his side of the story."

My friend followed my advice (even better, I should confess, than I sometimes follow my own advice). As it turned out, the son had been at a friend's house. The boy's father had stocked the refrigerator with beer and told the boys to enjoy themselves. Then he went upstairs and paid no attention to them the rest of the evening.

In essence, the father had put his stamp of approval on teenagers drinking beer in his family room. My friend realized that he and his son were up against a conflict between the values of the two families. One father, who considered himself an understanding, caring parent, thought he was providing good entertainment for a bunch of boys in his basement. It hadn't dawned on him that everyone except his son would have to drive home and might get in a wreck if they drank too much.

After talking to his son, my friend realized that the boy was really quite embarrassed about his behavior. Getting drunk wasn't as much fun as he thought it would be. In fact, he had gotten so sick physically from the alcohol and emotionally because he had violated his Christian standards that he had no intention of ever drinking again.

For my friend and his son this experience was one of their first times of real communication. The son was able to tell his dad that he sometimes felt their family was a bit stodgy and behind the times and that some of the rules didn't make any sense. He had thought that his friend's family was a lot more sophisticated and fun because they weren't so restrictive. But after this experience the son realized that his dad had some good reasons for not wanting him to drink. He realized that his family's standards weren't the result of a whimsical, arbitrary decision.

The son was not rebellious, he was simply curious. And so an evening that ended in drunkenness turned out to be a pivotal moment for this family.

--- --- --- --- ---

"Sometimes it takes a serious situation for parents to recognize the need to communicate."

--- --- --- --- ---

I could tell a hundred stories about situations like this, where only after conflict did a family begin to talk seriously and honestly about behavior. Sexual activity is another area that parents misinterpret as rebellion when it may be ignorance or curiosity.

Many parents find it difficult to discuss the realities of sexuality with their teenagers. Apparently not wanting to give their kids the idea that it is enjoyable, they give the impression that sex is somehow beneath them, or merely a duty.

One mother told me a story I could hardly believe, but it's not the kind of thing a person would make up. She and her husband went out for the evening and left their teenage daughter in charge of the other children. They returned earlier than expected. Their daughter's boyfriend's car was parked in the street, but when they went inside everything was quiet. No one in the kitchen. No one in the family room. No one in the living room.

Finally they found them—in the daughter's bedroom—in bed. The mother nearly passed out; the father raised his arm to hit someone; and the two kids scrambled to get their clothes on.

The father chased the frightened, half-dressed boyfriend out of the house, and the mother sat on the edge of the bed beside her sobbing daughter.

Though churning on the inside, the mother tried to remain calm as she soothed her daughter. When the girl finally was able to speak she said, "Well, at least you don't have to worry about me getting pregnant, Mom. We used protection."

"What did you use?" the mother asked, thinking the whole episode must have been premeditated if they'd had time to buy condoms.

"A sock," the daughter answered.

Despite all the warnings about safe sex, and despite all the sex-education classes in school, this girl had somehow gotten the idea that a nylon stocking would keep her from getting pregnant.

This kind of ignorance is almost inexcusable in our day, but I suspect it is not all that uncommon. Would information have kept the daughter from getting involved with her boyfriend? I doubt it. Would it have made it safer? Probably. But that is not the point of my story.

The point is that this mother and daughter had never talked about sex. The mother subconsciously thought, *If I don't tell her about sex, she won't find out how to do it.*

The daughter was probably thinking, *If sex were really something important my mother would have told me about it. I guess it won't hurt to try it and find out what it's all about.* Or she may have thought, *Maybe Mom is keeping sex a secret because she thinks I'll like it if I try it. If it's that much fun, why shouldn't I?*

Sometimes it takes a situation as serious as this for parents to recognize the need to communicate.

"The goal of parenting: children who can think clearly, take responsibility for their own actions, and have the will to learn from their mistakes."

Both of these stories had a happy ending. In each case forgiveness was offered, communication was improved, and there were no tragic consequences. The parents were able to start over with their children on a higher level of understanding. Although saddened by their child's loss of innocence, the parents were pleased that it had been replaced by knowledge that would provide a basis for clearheaded, honest discussion and decision making in the future.

And that is the goal of parenting: children who can think clearly, take responsibility for their own actions, and have the will to learn from their mistakes.

This Is the Way We Learn to Live

The best way to learn is from God Himself, through His Word and the authorities He places over us. Most of us are too stubborn to learn this way, however, so

God, in His graciousness, has an alternate plan. He teaches us through the consequences of our actions. No matter how serious our misbehavior, His offer of forgiveness and restoration is never withdrawn. He stands ready to give us a clean slate and another chance.

The beautiful thing about the Christian message is that it is often through conflict, crisis, and even failure that the best lessons are learned. We need spend only a few minutes reflecting on familiar Bible stories to validate this concept. For example, from Joseph's relationship with his brothers who sold him into slavery, we learn a great lesson of forgiveness and reconciliation. From David's sin of adultery with Bathsheba, we learn the limitlessness of God's forgiveness. From the apostle Paul, who participated in the martyrdom of Stephen, we learn how God can change even the most adamant opponent of Christianity.

All of these great lessons came out of difficulty, struggle, misunderstanding, and conflict. So it is probably unreasonable to expect that our teenagers will learn great lessons without pain and heartache. Sometimes, in fact, these are the only ways they can learn. Each family conflict has the potential to be the pivotal lesson that changes the direction of one or more family members.

My point is, even rebellion and failure can have positive results if we can see beyond our immediate disappointment and fear.

I am not fatalistic about the task of equipping young people to live responsible, productive lives as emotionally healthy adults. I believe the majority of kids raised in Christian families will lead worthwhile lives. We need only faith in ourselves as parents, faith in our children's ability to grasp what we teach them, and faith in God's promises.

—— 10 ——

Independently Healthy

PRINCIPLE 10

Give your teenagers bites of freedom.

I have spoken at hundreds of youth conventions, but one was different. It was the one my daughter attended for the first time. She was a freshman in high school and had decided that she wanted to go with her friends and be part of the Youth for Christ Capital Teen Convention we were holding in Washington, D.C.

I had spent twenty years in Youth for Christ ministry and had sponsored hundreds of events with tens of thousands of young people all over the world. But for the first time my own daughter was going to participate.

I was nervous, afraid I wouldn't do a good enough job. For the first time I felt old. Suddenly I wondered if I had any business being in youth work at my age. I didn't want somebody sitting next to her to say, "Who is that old guy trying to talk to kids? Why doesn't he go play shuffleboard?" So I was very conscious about doing the best job I could. At the same time, I was anxious that she have her independence and not be tied to me. It was a very complicated family dynamic for me.

I flew in late in the afternoon and was supposed to give the keynote address to the thirty-five hundred young people gathered there. When I arrived at the hotel, I immediately went to my room. Then, as I always do, I went to the window to check out the view. Below me were hundreds of kids milling around the hotel entry. I hadn't been watching for a minute when I spotted my daughter and her friend. From ten stories up, out of hundreds of kids dressed just alike, I picked her out. No sooner had I spotted her, however, than I noticed that she was walking in the wrong direction. Supper was over and it was time for everyone to be heading to the convention center to hear me speak. Surely she hadn't decided to skip my session, had she?

I watched a few more seconds before it dawned on me that not only was she walking away from where she should be going, she was walking toward a particular part of town where I would not want to walk alone, much less have my daughter walk.

I panicked. *My goodness*, I thought, *she doesn't understand where she's supposed to go. She doesn't realize the danger she's in.* I had to speak at the meeting in just a few minutes, so I couldn't run after her. In desperation I phoned a friend who is a staff member and said, "I just saw Laurie and her friend heading in the wrong direction. I hate to be the over-concerned parent, but would you check it out for me?" He promised he would, so I left for the meeting, though still very uncomfortable about the situation, and met my friends. While watching thousands of kids enter the hall to hear me speak, the only one I could think about was the one who was missing.

"Few parents question the value of building independence in children, but the actual process of letting go is a great deal more difficult than talking about it."

A few minutes after the meeting began, the staff member I had called entered the back door of the auditorium and signaled to me that everything was all right. I sighed with relief and got through my message, though still trembling inside.

I later learned that Laurie's friend had left her purse at a fast-food restaurant down the street and they were simply going back to get it. The staff member had caught up with them and walked along. They never found the purse, but the girls made it back safely, thinking it was just a coincidence that the staff member had shown up.

Few parents question the value of building independence in children, but the actual process of letting go is a great deal more difficult than talking about it. I can still recall the terrible fear I felt when my daughter had that first (at least to my knowledge) independent life experience. I wasn't thinking about the 3,499 other kids who had been entrusted to us by their parents for this convention. Nor the tens of thousands, perhaps hundreds of thousands, who had been entrusted to us at camps to do everything from play softball and baseball to climb mountains, spelunk, water-ski, trampoline, repel off cliffs, and canoe white-water rapids. All of the potentially dangerous things we do in youth work had hardly given me a second thought until it involved my own daughter. Then suddenly I felt the emotion all parents feel.

So here I am, writing to you, saying you have to let go, you have to let your children have independent experiences, but as I do so I acknowledge that there is a price you will have to pay for it: frequent stomach distress and sleepless nights.

The question is, Do we build fences around our kids and not let them have these experiences because the risks are too great (and our stomachs can't stand the upset)?

Of course not. We allow them to have the experiences and we go out and stock up on stomach medication for all those Maalox moments ahead of us.

In addition, however, there are things we can do to minimize the risks. We can warn them about the dangers in the world.

Parents have a natural instinct for warning kids about danger, and they don't waste any time getting started. "Don't put that bug in your mouth." "Don't ride your bike in the street." "Don't talk to strangers." "Don't do something just because all your friends do it." "Don't be gullible." "Don't get separated from the rest of the group."

When the kids get a little older, our words of wisdom change from commands to deep philosophical thoughts. "You don't have to eat mud to know it doesn't taste good." "If Junior jumped headfirst off a skyscraper, would you do the same thing?" "I don't care if Captain Kangaroo himself said it; it's not true." "If Susie told you she has three belly buttons, would you believe her?"

Your kids can probably repeat your pet phrases verbatim, and that's good. They know what's smart and what's not. Now, if there were just some guarantee that they would always make the smart choice. There is no such thing, of course, but we can make smart choices easier for them to choose: We can put them in the care of people we trust.

A church youth program run by mature adults supplies more relief than a lifetime supply of Maalox. The difference? It will help you to manage the risks instead of just survive them. A good youth program allows your kids maximum opportunities for adventure with minimum risk. Some parents ignore the resources available in the local church and miss a great opportunity. A good youth program can take a lot of anxiety out of the task of parenting. Many youth programs provide high-adventure opportunities that help young people grow toward independence in an environment that makes it easier for parents to let go.

"Kids will find adventure. We can either plan it for them, or we can worry and fret about what they'll come up with on their own."

Our children, for example, were involved in the Wandering Wheels Program started by former football star Bob Davenport. Thirty-five or forty kids from our youth group, along with three or four sponsors, would take off in a bus with the seats taken out so the kids could sleep on the floor in sleeping bags.

Two or three drivers took turns at the wheel so the kids could sleep all night and awaken the next morning in some exciting place. There would be planned activities for the day, then everyone would get back on the bus, sleep for another eight hours, and wake up in another place. Our kids went to the Smoky Mountains, Washington, D.C., Gettysburg, Niagara Falls, the Grand Canyon, and Disney World like this. These kinds of programs are available through Campus Life, Young Life, Student Venture, and many other evangelical youth programs.

Sometimes I hear parents say these are indulgent, that we're spending a lot of money on these programs and kids don't appreciate them. When I hear comments like this, I think of some of the alternatives. The fact is, kids will find adventure. We can either plan it for them, something they will enjoy, or we can worry and fret about what they'll come up with on their own.

Personally, I would rather have my kids chugging down the road at fifty-five miles an hour with a busload of teenagers singing gospel choruses than speeding down the expressway with a few friends going to the beach or a ball game. I've been passed on the highway by a car full of young fellows going twenty miles over the speed limit and passing cans of beer from one to another. They have found adventure, all right, but it's not the kind I want for my kids.

Teenagers are a lot less likely to get into serious trouble on a bus crammed with kids going off to a planned event with a youth pastor than with a few peers who are as immature and inexperienced as they are. I would be willing to spend a good deal of the church's resources to make fun-filled, adventure-packed, minimal-risk opportunities available for young people today.

These kinds of activities are the ideal mix between being realistic about the dangers of a modern world and being aware of the need to develop independence in our kids. We are not tossing them to the wolves, as it were, or saying, "Let the fittest survive," in some Darwinian sort of way.

On the other hand, we are not treating them like hothouse plants that never get climatized to the real world. Yes, things do happen on these trips. Yes, kids do things adults don't approve of. Yes, there may be some who sneak alcohol or find an opportunity for illicit sexual behavior. However, because of the presence of counselors and staff, these escapades usually don't get to the level of danger they would reach in an unchaperoned environment. Risks are inevitable, but they are limited when there is adult supervision.

—·—·—·—·—·—·—

"I would never suggest that Christian parents be more permissive than their

non-Christian peers, but it is ironic that so many of us worry more."

Another way to entrust your children to the care of other adults is to make friends with couples who have children the same age as yours. For instance, in a church where there are fifteen or twenty couples whose kids are all the same age, there are a variety of ways you can help each other with the parenting task. Families that have swimming pools, lake houses, ski boats, or other types of recreational facilities usually are willing to take one or two additional teens along when they use them.

If my fourteen-year-old daughter wants to learn to water-ski, I would love to have her taught by a friend from church who has a daughter the same age and is teaching them both at the same time. Though I am apprehensive about all the dangers connected with water sports, my heart is at ease with the knowledge that this man will do nothing with my daughter that he would not do with his own. So she goes away for the weekend and water-skis until she gets such a blistering sunburn that she can't go to school on Monday morning. As parents, we're not exactly pleased, but she has had an adventurous weekend. She has shown her independence, is alive to tell about it, and has suffered no permanent damage.

The whole time these friends of mine are helping me with my daughter's search for independence, they are enjoying their family life together. This is reciprocal, of course. We do this sort of thing with our friends' children as well.

These are the types of experiences and adventures kids need if they are going to become self-reliant young people, independent of their parents.

We can also surround our teens with lots of prayer. You may think that the parents of some of your children's friends already give their kids too much freedom. They let them go places and do things where they are unsupervised much of the time. This may be true, but Christians are more likely to have the opposite problem. We tend to be overly protective because we know too much about the dangers in the world, are too concerned about the safety of our offspring, and, in general, don't have enough trust in them, ourselves, or the Lord.

Finding the balance is tough for parents. And I am sure the balance is different for every single family and for every individual child within every family.

I would never suggest that Christian parents be more permissive than their non-Christian peers, but it is ironic that so many of us worry more. We have advantages over non-Christians that should give us great confidence in child rearing. One of those advantages is prayer. We can call upon the Lord daily to protect our children from the influences and experiences we cannot control.

"Self-imposed restrictions are always more effective than restrictions imposed by others."

Friends of ours have a daughter who wanted to cross the state line with her friends and go to a dance club where all the kids were hanging out. She had never done it but kept begging to go, insisting it was absolutely necessary for her social well-being. She begged and pleaded, pleaded and begged. Eventually her mom and dad said, "Okay, you can go, but you've got to promise to behave yourself and live by our family standards." They gave her the obligatory lecture that we always give our kids when they are about to do something we don't approve of.

So she got in the car with four of her girlfriends and they drove the forty miles to this wonderful, magical place where they could enjoy some adventure and finally live like grownups. Her parents waved goodbye, went inside, made coffee, sat across from each other at the dining room table, and prepared themselves for the long, anxious hours until 1 A.M.

At 11:30 their daughter showed up.

"What in the world are you doing home?" the father asked. "I thought you were going to stay there until midnight and then drive home."

"Dad, you're never going to believe this, but we really learned a lesson tonight. We wanted to have some fun and be like the other kids. We even wanted to be a little wild. But we never wanted to be that wild. That place was a meat market. It was just awful the way the girls were acting and the way they were being treated by the guys. I wouldn't hang around there for anything. I don't ever want to go to a place like that again."

What a great lesson for both the parents and the daughter. The daughter learned that some of the activities glamorized on television really aren't all that much fun and, in fact, involve a lot of humiliating, degrading behavior. And the parents learned that they could trust their daughter, that all their warnings, guidance, discipline, and prayers had been effective. Not only did she dislike the seamy side of life, she even came home and admitted to them that she found it abominable.

Parents with a daughter like that don't have a lot to worry about. From now on they will know that she can set her own limits. And that is the breakthrough every parent hopes for because self-imposed restrictions are always more effective than restrictions imposed by others.

But suppose she had liked what she found there and had gotten into trouble—what then? That is a risk every parent inevitably will face. Either you yourself can choose the best time and occasion to allow your children to take the risk or you can wait until they choose it for themselves.

Look at it another way. Suppose they had not allowed her to go. She would never have known she didn't like it, and they would never have had the peace of mind of knowing she didn't like it. As I mentioned earlier, you have to have faith in the building material you have used, in the foundation you have laid for your children.

A further complication of letting go that parents (especially fathers of daughters) find difficult to accept is the loss of innocence. Most of us equate naiveté with purity. In other words, they are pure if they don't know certain things and, conversely, they are not pure if they do know certain things. To equate the loss of purity with the loss of innocence in this way is a mistake. We need to discuss with them the things we can't protect them from.

"To equate the loss of purity with the loss of innocence is a mistake."

When our children were young we lived directly across the street from an elementary-school playground and our children went across the street to play on the swings and slides anytime they wanted to. It was almost like an extension of our front yard.

One day word came that there had been a flasher on the playground exposing himself to little girls. I became incensed, angry. In fact, I discovered things about my own personality I didn't even know were there. I was so angry I could have choked him. Then I began to think about my own girls, who were about five and eight at the time, and wondered what they had seen, what conclusions they had drawn from what they had seen, and what they knew about what they had seen.

I was distraught by my complete inability to take away knowledge they were too young to have. They had lost their innocence too soon, and I began to feel as if they had lost purity at the same time. But I was wrong. Although I mourned their loss of innocence, they had not lost their purity.

As they grew older I realized that song lyrics, television programs, books, magazines, and things passed around on the playground had made them aware of things usually associated with the twisted and bent side of human behavior.

Parents—especially parents of teenagers—have to come to terms with this. Like it or not, in our free and open society, our young people will inevitably come in contact with things we'd like to keep from them. The only thing a parent can do is to contextualize these experiences so our kids know that they have a moral choice as to whether they will accept or reject such behavior.

To be aware of such behavior does not make us guilty of having committed it. And to deny its existence—to drive it underground, make it sneaky or clandestine—gives it a power it doesn't deserve or possess. As Proverbs 9:17 says, "Stolen water is sweet; food eaten in secret is delicious!" Certain ideas, when not exposed to the daylight, when not examined with a clear mind, have more power than if we allow them into the open. When darkness is exposed to light, however, it ceases to exist.

Part of letting go is realizing that our teenagers are going to come into contact with words, ideas, habits, and behaviors that are not only sinful but perverted. We must be willing to openly discuss these things with our kids so that it takes away the powerful feeling they get of "Hey, I know something my parents don't know. Boy, are they naive."

_____

"Certain ideas, when not exposed to the daylight, have more power than if we allow them into the open. When darkness is exposed to light, it ceases to exist."

_____

By bringing certain subjects out into the open, even though they're not our favorite subjects for discussion, we can expose them for what they are, show the weakness they really possess, and reveal the unhappiness they bring. I am speaking of such things as drunkenness, sexual perversions, and occult practices. The media often romanticize these things and make them seem normal, if not appealing. But when discussed openly they become what they really are—the expressions of confused people.

The Madonna video that takes place in a church is an example. It combines the symbolism of the crucifix with her sensuous movements in a way I consider offensive. These images are given power by their very outrageousness. A woman going through sexual gyrations at the foot of the cross, apparently as some kind of sacrifice, flaunts evil in a way that is a step beyond the usual expression of rebellion.

Can you forbid your teenagers to watch it? Yes. Can you guarantee that they won't see it at a friend's house? No. About the only thing you can do to protect your teens from the influences of this kind of stuff is to watch it yourself (or listen to it if it's music). This probably is not your favorite thing to do, but you've got to be able to respond with a comment more intelligent than "What? You watched that vulgar thing? Where's your brain anyway? Haven't you listened to anything we've told you?"

A better response would be: "What did you think of it? Maybe I'd better watch it too so we can discuss it. Would you like to watch it again with me?"

The answer probably will be "No thanks," but don't let that keep you from following through. Rent it or wait for it to show up on MTV again, but watch it. Then wait for a good opportunity to discuss it. Don't start out with some loaded question like "Why do people enjoy things that are so perverted?" or a close-ended question like "Have you ever seen anything so sacrilegious in your life?"

Instead, ask something like, "Why do you suppose she chose a church for the setting?" or "What is she saying about Jesus when she does that?" As young people confront and discuss these images they begin to see them for what they really are.

Parents really have no choice as to whether or not they let kids go in this sense. Bad influences are everywhere, and there is no way to keep kids away from them. The choice we do have is how we will influence the way our kids interpret all this negative input.

The fact is, teenagers have and need more freedom than children do. Parents must get used to the idea and realize that freedom can be a great teacher. It has now become commonplace for churches, youth organizations, and colleges to sponsor travel to places in the United States like theme parks or to more substantial places like other countries to do social work, build facilities, or evangelize. The very idea of allowing a teenager to travel to a foreign country brings terror to many parents. I have been responsible for thousands of these experiences for kids in Youth for Christ and now at Taylor University. Is there danger? Yes, certainly, there is some. Will they see things that shock, frighten, or challenge them? Again, yes. Under proper adult supervision, however, I believe that these experiences can teach lessons that years of school, reading, movies, television, or the World Wide Web will never teach. Kids see the results of injustice, they develop gratitude for family and country, they see the treasure of Christian values in contrast to the rites of paganism and other religions. They buy foolish things, get gypped by vendors, develop pen pals, but mostly they are stretched toward adulthood far beyond most of us when we were their age.

As a result they reflect for the rest of their lives on the experiences they had. They develop a point of reference and an expanded worldview. If these experiences seem financially beyond reach or unavailable, families can provide growth experiences together.

"Bad influences are everywhere, and there is no way to keep kids away from them. The choice we do have is how we will influence the way our kids interpret all this negative input."

Summer vacations are a great time to allow your teenagers to do some independent things. Choose an environment that is fun and safe and give them as much freedom as you dare.

It is good to help our kids measure themselves against others and see how they are doing in the world of independent living. We can provide opportunities for them to test their independence. Canoeing was the activity that helped my son and me do this. We went on father-and-son canoe trips to test our relationship. Did I give him as much independence as the other dads gave their sons? How did I handle discipline problems compared to how they handled theirs? Did we respect each other as much as the other fathers and sons? How did we do in working out problems together?

Each of our canoe trips taught us something from observing others. Sometimes we learned how to do something; sometimes we learned how not to do something. If we saw someone do something particularly stupid, we would discuss a better way of doing it when we were paddling alone.

"Young people with parents who provide opportunities to take little trips away from the nest will gain independence and insights into their own personalities."

Sometimes, of course, even parents have problems taking advice and handling independent experiences. When kids observe this, it will help them realize that maturity doesn't automatically come with age.

On one particular Campus Life canoe trip everyone was warned not to get out into the deep water because the waves were high. The guide even described how they would turn a canoe over and over like some kind of roller on a washing machine, dumping all your stuff into the lake in the process. Even though supposedly mature dads were on board, a couple of canoes went where they didn't belong and ended up going over and over and losing their gear in the middle of the water. Both dads and sons had to admit they had gone beyond the boundaries and ignored good advice. The lessons to be learned from these situations are not restricted to young people.

Young people with parents who provide opportunities to take little trips away from the nest will gain independence and insights into their own personalities. If they come back hurt, the parents can help them understand what happened, show them how to correct what went wrong, and send them out again.

The idea is to keep pushing them farther and farther away until eventually they don't have to come back because they can stand alone as emotionally healthy young adults. Later, however, they will look back and say, "Those were wonderful experiences you gave us, Mom and Dad. We had the chance to develop our own identity but still be part of the family. Thanks."

Passing the Baton

Only Want to Be Free

*I*t wasn't that Sam didn't like his father. He did. In fact, everybody liked him. He was a really nice guy. Perhaps that was even part of the problem. Maybe he was just too nice. He always let people walk all over him. If his customers didn't pay their bills he always gave them the benefit of the doubt. If one of his workers didn't show up, he'd pitch in and do the guy's work. Sam wondered how his dad could be so gullible when he heard the flimsy excuses people gave. And the church he went to—that was another story. All the "do unto others" stuff they talked about there didn't seem to be helping any of the people. They all stayed poor no matter how nice they were or how hard they worked.

After high school Sam decided it was time to take matters into his own hands. If his dad was ever going to get enough money in the bank to retire, he was going to need some help.

Finally he approached his father with his plan. He wanted to take the money saved for his college education and invest it in a foolproof plan that his best friend's brother had been telling them about. Russ had even invited Sam to join his investment firm. Not a bad offer for a kid just out of high school. Russ must have seen real potential in him.

Russ himself was making money hand over fist. Sam knew it was true because of the car he drove— it even had a phone in it—and the pictures he'd shown them of his house in the city. Russ told Sam he could get started with just a little bit of cash. Sam was somewhat surprised to find out that what Russ considered "a little bit" was Sam's total college education fund. But if he could double it in a year or two, everybody would come out ahead. He could still go to college, and his father could retire before he worked himself to death.

Sam could tell that his father wasn't as excited about the idea as he was, so he started laying on the guilt. "You're always giving, giving, giving to everyone else," he said. "But you won't even give your own son what is rightfully his. You've always treated everyone else better than me. It's not fair."

Sam knew that being fair was one of his father's highest ideals. If the man had any pride at all it was in the fact that he always went the extra mile. Never had he knowingly treated anyone unfairly. In fact, if he ever heard that anyone even thought he had been unfair, he would do whatever he could to make it right.

Somehow realizing that his father's greatest strength was also his greatest weakness, Sam took advantage of it. And it worked. By the end of the week he had a check in his hand for the whole amount.

Within a few months, Sam started receiving dividends just like Russ had promised. Russ advised him not to put any of it in the bank just yet. "Spend some of it on yourself," he suggested. "You've got to raise your standard of living if you're ever going to get people to trust you with their money. Appearances are very important to the people we deal with. Then, whatever money's left you should reinvest."

Sam followed Russ's advice. After all, it was obviously working for him. Why argue? Besides, Russ had been right in his assessment of Sam. He was learning quickly and fitting in well. He was meeting people he'd read about in newspapers, eating at restaurants whose chefs were as famous as the clients, and dating girls who'd been on the covers of magazines. What a life.

Sam kept in touch with his family and friends back home. He wasn't becoming a snob or anything, and he didn't want anyone to think of him that way. But it was getting harder and harder to talk to them. They had no idea what the real world was like. Conversations with his dad kept getting shorter and shorter, but he always ended them the same way. "In just a little while longer I'll have enough money to come home, Dad," he'd say. "Then you can retire, you and Mom can travel, and I can go to college. Everything is working out just like I planned."

The last call Ed got from his son Sam was three months ago. Sam hadn't given even a hint that anything was wrong. In fact, he said the same thing he always said—that he'd be home in just a few months. Well, a few months had come and gone with no word at all from Sam. That just wasn't like him. He had called every week or two since leaving home. But now when Ed called his son, he always got Sam's answering machine. When he wrote, his letters were never answered.

Ed began to get concerned. He didn't say much about it because he didn't want to alarm his wife, but he knew that she too would soon begin to get suspicious. The stuff he was reading in the newspapers did not sound good. Things weren't going well in the investment business. Many old, stable companies were verging on bankruptcy, and many newer ones had already gone under. Sam's firm was never mentioned, but Ed couldn't imagine how anything so new and small could survive the upheaval.

One day when Ed tried to call he didn't get the

answering machine; he got something even worse—
a recording that said the number had been discon-
nected. Ed was sure then that the worst had happened.
Sam had lost everything and was too ashamed to tell
his dad. Two powerful forces went to work in Ed. One
tugged at him to go buy an airplane ticket, find his
son, and bring him home where he belonged. The
other force held him back. The voice of the second
reminded him, "Your son wanted what was his and
you gave it to him. He wanted his freedom and you
gave it to him. His life is no longer yours. You can't
take it back no matter how foolishly you think he used
it. He's got to decide what to do next. And you've got
to wait."

Ed knew the voice was right, but every fatherly
instinct he had in him pleaded with him to ignore it.
Ed pondered every conversation he'd ever had with
Sam, every activity they'd ever done together, every
harsh word he'd ever spoken, every disciplinary action
he'd ever enforced. Had he been too strict? Not strict
enough?

Months passed, and the forces inside him continued
their fight, leaving him tired, distracted, even irritable.
He began to hear rumors about how Sam was earning a living, but he didn't want to believe any of them.
All he knew was that he wanted to restore his relationship with his son, no matter what he had done.

Ed stayed home as much as possible to be near

the phone. He checked the mail as soon as it came. He worked a lot in the front yard so he could watch the cars go by. He was afraid that if Sam did come home he might lose his nerve before coming into the driveway. Ed wanted to be there to meet him to make sure that didn't happen.

Finally his waiting paid off. After spending a hot Saturday morning at work in his flower beds, Ed stood up to admire his garden and wipe his forehead. He was just about to go into the house to get something cold to drink when he spotted a taxi a few blocks up the street. That was not a common sight. There was no need for taxis in their small town. Everything was within walking distance. In fact, Ed had never even seen a taxi anywhere in town, much less on their street.

He pushed the gate open and started up the sidewalk, shading his eyes from the sun so he could see better. The taxi approached slowly and stopped abruptly when it reached Ed. The back door opened. Ed squinted so he could see inside, but the glint of the sun on the trim of the cab blinded him. He moved closer and saw the passenger pay the driver.

For a moment Ed thought his knees were going to give out and he was going to fall to the pavement in a heap. He didn't know if it was from kneeling too long in the garden or from the joy of seeing his son once again. He'd never felt so weak.

"Thank You, God," Ed mumbled as he grabbed his

son and embraced him with every bit of strength left in his feeble arms. It felt so good to have a real body to hold instead of just a mental picture. The energy that passed between father and son restored Ed's strength.

"I'm sorry, Dad, so sorry," Sam whispered.

"Thank You, God," Ed said again. "And God bless you, son. Everything's going to be all right now." And Ed knew it would be. His son had made a bad decision, but he'd had the courage to admit it. And then he'd had the sense to make a right decision, and a very difficult one it was. In the back of Ed's mind was the thought that Sam had probably learned more from this difficult experience than any college could have taught him, but such thoughts would have to wait.

As the taxi disappeared in the distance, Sam and Ed started home. They had so much to talk about, but neither could find the words. For now their actions would have to do all the talking.

There comes a time in every parent/child relationship when parents must pass the baton of life to their child and let the child go on ahead, whether or not they think the child is ready. They can't wait until they're sure the track ahead is smooth and safe; no one can see far enough ahead. They can't wait until they've been around every turn together; the track of life keeps changing. They can't wait for their child to stop stumbling; even the best runners sometimes lose their footing. And they can't wait for their child to be in perfect step with them; every runner has his or her own pace and style.

All parents hope this transitional period won't be as difficult for them as it was for Ed, but for some it will be. Ed was a good father. He lived a good life, a clean life, a simple life. Perhaps he was a bit too naive and trusting, but that's no sin. He did nothing to "deserve" a wayward son. Neither did God, of course, but He certainly has His share of wayward children.

Was it wrong for Ed to give Sam money? No. God the Father gives believers their inheritance to spend as they see fit. Was it wrong for Ed to give Sam freedom? No. God the Father gives His children freedom to follow at His side or go their own way. Was it wrong for Ed to welcome Sam back after he had acted so foolishly and irresponsibly? No. God the Father is always waiting to reconcile His wandering children.

"Trust is far more effective in motivating good behavior than are distrust and suspicion."

The point that needs to be made here is that God the Father gives His children a great deal of freedom. Apparently there is a need for individuals to learn the consequences of decisions by being allowed to make foolish ones. If our heavenly Parent has chosen to treat His creation in this manner, it seems reasonable to conclude that we should follow His example in our relationships with our kids, even though there are risks involved.

Ed had no guarantee that Sam wouldn't get into irreversible trouble when he let his son follow his dream. Neither does God when He gives us freedom. Ed had no guarantee that Sam would not stubbornly refuse to return home even when his life began to fall apart. Neither does God when we go our own selfish way. Ed had no guarantee that Sam would survive life in the fast lane.

Neither does God when we choose the excitement of this world over the joys of His. Yet God the Father takes the risk. Apparently the lessons to be learned are of great value.

Of course, there are no guarantees the other way either. That is, we cannot guarantee good behavior by restraining children any more than we can guarantee it by trusting them to go free. However, working with young people over the course of my lifetime has taught me that trust is far more effective in motivating good behavior than are distrust and suspicion.

Fortunately, failure does not mean the end of the world. It may mean loss of money or resources, but apparently the heavenly Father considers the money well spent if the lessons learned bring the child back home.

"One of the central tenets of the Christian faith is this very point—that God, having let us go our own way when we chose disobedience, waits for our return, eager to help us start life over again."

It may mean loss of freedom if it involves criminal behavior and results in imprisonment. It may mean loss of health if it involves alcohol, drugs, or promiscuity and results in accident or illness. It may mean loss of opportunity if it involves sexual activity and results in a teenage pregnancy that requires the young mother and/or father to go to work instead of college.

But I've known young people who've been through these failures, learned from them, turned their lives over to God, and gone on to become wonderful, responsible adults. Fortunately, not all mistakes are as costly and painful as those that involve breaking the law, sexual experimentation, drinking alcohol, or taking drugs. However, the power of Christ is such that even things this severe can be overcome by the grace of God. This is especially true if parents understand the concept of the waiting father and provide for their children a haven, a place where they can find a new beginning, rebirth, and a chance to redeem their lives after failure.

One of the central tenets of the Christian faith is this very point—that God, having given us the freedom to make choices and having let us go our own way when we chose disobedience, waits for our return, eager to help us start life over again.

Thus far I've discussed only the frightening part of passing the baton, but there's also an exhilarating part as well. When we see our children running smoothly at our side, keeping our pace, it is time to pass the baton and let them go for it. When we do, we may be surprised to see that they can run faster and smoother than we ever could.

In my position as a college president, I have the privilege of seeing a great many young adults living independently from their parents, and I am convinced that many of them will move far beyond where their parents ever dreamed of going in obedience and commitment to the Lord. A great many young people today are looking at the Christian faith with greater seriousness than did previous generations and are deeply committed to make their lives count for Christ. I believe they are more committed to shared responsibility in marriage, in parenting, and in working together to build strong families. They have seen the ravages of materialism and they are eager to build their lives on solid family values and Christian principles.

Having seen our kids change from dependent children to independent adults so that we now enjoy a new relationship with them as peers is the most rewarding experience of our lives. And to stand on the sidelines and watch our kids achieve things we couldn't quite reach is the greatest joy of parenthood.

God bless you in your role as parent. My best prayer for you is that parenting will be as rewarding and fulfilling for you as it has been for Janie and me, and that you too will experience the joys of raising emotionally healthy teenagers.

Index

About the Author

*D*R. JAY KESLER is president of Taylor University, an interdenominational Christian undergraduate institution in Upland, Indiana. Founded in 1846, Taylor has more than seventeen hundred students. Dr. Kesler is a best-selling author in the field of family life. He has written many books, including *Ten Mistakes Parents Make with Teenagers (And How to Avoid Them)*, Wolgemuth & Hyatt (1989). He and his wife, Janie, have three children, Laurie, Bruce, and Terri, and nine grandchildren.

After earning his undergraduate degree from Taylor University, Dr. Kesler received doctoral degrees from Barrington College, Taylor University, Huntington College, Asbury Theological Seminary, and John Brown University. Dr. Kesler has a long history of youth work and service with many organizations.